Satan on the Loose

Satan
on the
Loose

Nicky Cruz

FLEMING H. REVELL COMPANY
Old Tappan, New Jersey

ISBN 0   8007   0574   2

Copyright © 1973 by Nicky Cruz
Published by Fleming H. Revell Company
Library of Congress Catalog Card Number: 73-1125
All Rights Reserved
Printed in the United States of America

TO my mother
once trapped in witchcraft —
now liberated forever

ACKNOWLEDGMENTS

Heartfelt thanks go to these wonderful Christians without whom this book could not have been written: To Lana and Lou Rawls who spent many hours taping their experiences, and then allowing these experiences to be revealed . . . To Julio Ruibal whose personal account has added so much to SATAN ON THE LOOSE . . . To Jeanie Weyant and Janice Andrews, my hardworking and efficient secretaries, who prepared many pages of material . . . And finally, to my wonderful wife, Gloria, and our three daughters — Alicia, Laura, and Nicole — for their loving patience with me as I worked far into the night.

Contents

Be sober, be vigilant; because your adversary the devil, as a roaring lion, walketh about, seeking whom he may devour: whom resist stedfast in the faith. . . .   1 Peter 5:8, 9

> For still our ancient foe
> Doth seek to work us woe;
> His craft and power are great,
> And, armed with cruel hate,
> On earth is not his equal.
>   Martin Luther

If one believes in the truth of the Bible, it is impossible to doubt the reality of the devil for a single instant.
                                    Denis de Rougemont

The devil's cleverest wile is to make men believe that he does not exist.   Gerald C. Treacy

Satan on the Loose

1

Into the Darkness

Strange things are stirring in the world now. Anyone can feel it.

It hits you all of a sudden — it did me, anyway. I was flying to Chicago when a dark fog began to settle down over my spirit. It was bright enough outside. The sun made the farms and fields down below as bright as a picture book, and the sky was blue, but I felt a strange unrest as we zeroed in toward O'Hare airport.

It was silly, I told myself. I had more speaking engagements than I could fill; young people all over the country were finding hope and liberation through my work; I had just signed a contract for a new book; I had the loveliest family and the most exciting opportunities I could hope for — but I felt depressed.

"Snap out of it, Nicky," I told myself. "You've got everything going for you — plus God!"

I felt more depressed than ever.

There was no explanation for it at all. The closer we got to the airport the worse I felt. It was a kind of pall I couldn't fight off.

Jesus, help me! I pleaded in desperation, but there was no answer. He seemed far away.

My spiritual depression lifted an inch or two when I found John Ambrose, a sales executive and friend of many years, waiting for me at O'Hare. As I settled down for the long ride to our destination, I thanked God for John and all the other brothers and sisters in Christ who make my work possible.

Seeing John reminded me of the first time I had spoken in his city, and of some of the great young people who had helped make that earlier crusade successful.

"How's Leif?" I asked.

Leif Nyborg was one of those big, husky, handsome fellows who make everybody feel good. A football quarterback with blond hair and blue eyes, Leif always had a dozen fellows and girls around him. The first night of my first crusade, he brought along all the young people in his church and it seemed like half the youngsters in his high school. Leif was the kind of natural leader every pastor prays he'll find. The last time I'd seen John, Leif and five carloads of young people had come with him to the airport to see me off.

John sighed as we headed out Route 94. "I haven't seen much of Leif lately. He's into reincarnation now."

"He's what?" I asked.

"He's into reincarnation. You know—believing you keep coming back to earth over and over after you die."

Deep in my mind a memory was stirring. I couldn't quite place where I had heard something like this before, but it sounded bad. The sense of foreboding increased. I had a feeling of something as unclean as the dirty-looking waters of Lake Michigan on our left.

John went on: "Leif started talking about astrology a few months ago—sun signs and planetary influences and all that. He says the Wise Men were astrologers—which may be, for all I know—but I don't like the way he talks these days. For a while he was making a big thing of Jesus being a Capricorn, I think he said, and the next thing I knew Leif was talking about Christ as an Ascended Master. He seems to think Jesus is a master—not *the* Master—because He made it through other incarnations until He reached perfection. Only Leif says everyone has to keep coming back till we become Ascended Masters, too."

Now I really felt depressed. "How are the other young people coming along?" I asked.

John shook his head. "A lot of them are beginning to talk the way Leif does. By the way, do you remember Olga Santiri?"

I tried to place the name.

"I would be surprised if you did remember her, really. She's one of the girls in our church that never made much of an impression on anyone. But she phoned twice yesterday—says she's got to see you."

We were just starting dinner at the Ambrose home when the phone rang and the voice that came over it was so insistent that in spite of travel fatigue I agreed to see Olga that evening. John and his wife left us alone in the living room as she poured out her story.

Olga, a tall, thin girl who looked about eighteen, kept clasping and unclasping her hands as she talked. "I don't know what to do, Mr. Cruz," she said in a dead voice.

"Call me Nicky," I said. "What is the problem?"

The story that poured out of those pale lips shook me. Olga's father had left home years before. Her mother had recently been doing some strange things. She had redecorated their basement recreation room in what Olga called a "spooky" manner, and every few weeks either her mother was away for much of the night, or "her weird friends" met in her basement.

"Weird?" I asked. I knew how turned-off young people can get by their parents these days.

"Yes, I mean weird!" Olga said in a voice that was beginning to get sharper and higher-pitched. "You should see the way they look, Nicky. Two of those men look like the devil himself. And the sounds and smells that fill the house when they meet in our basement."

"Olga," I said, "that sounds a lot like the way some parents talk to me about their children."

"But this is *different*," she said. "They met at our house about two weeks ago. I was baby-sitting, but I got home early and when my mother heard me come in she rushed upstairs with the funniest look on her face—more like a kid that's been caught doing something bad. But she finally said, 'You're a big girl now, Olga, and there are some things you might as well learn.'

"Mother told me to come down to the basement," Olga went on, "and there were at least a dozen people there. It was something like a church service—only backwards. I mean backwards, Nicky. They said the Lord's Prayer backwards. Mother had fixed up a sort of altar with black candles on it and there was a cross hung on the wall behind it—upside down!

"Nicky, they read some awful things out of a black book and they said some prayers—not to God but to spirits with weird names. I remember one prayer was to Lucifer. There was some 'spirit of ancient power' they called on to 'come up from the fiery depths' and I think he came, Nicky. There was a moment after that when everything was as quiet as a tomb, and then you could feel something wicked coming into the basement. There was a lot of incense burning, and I think some people were smoking pot. I'm not sure now, but the air seemed to get thicker and darker and I could see a change coming into different people's faces.

"Someone started a crazy record playing. My mother took her shoes off, different people took some of their clothes off, and one woman and two men took off everything, and they all started dancing around and around the room. Some of them started barking like dogs.

"I noticed one of the men kept looking at me in a funny way and all of a sudden he grabbed my wrists and forced me to go off into a dark corner. . . ."

Olga started to sob and it broke my heart. I prayed for words to help her.

"He hurt me, Nicky!" she sobbed. "He was like a mad dog—only worse! Then two other men came over—I'm so ashamed I wish I was dead!"

"Does your mother know what happened?" I asked.

"Of course she knows! I think she's glad! I heard her on the phone once talking to someone about her 'goody-goody,' and I think she believes in one of the prayers they made that night. *Evil be my good.* Nicky, I don't think those people would stop at anything."

God gave me words I never could have thought of by myself, words that brought some measure of comfort to a badly bruised little heart. We asked John Ambrose and his wife to come in and join us in prayer that Olga might find again the Lord's forgiveness and joy, and His deliverance from evil.

That night I tossed and turned hour after hour. I seethed with anger at Olga's mother and the men who had raped this innocent girl. I felt sick about Leif, who had the potential of becoming a terrific Christian leader. I thought about the future.

People have often asked me, "What do you think about the Jesus People movement?" I think it's the work of God that many of us have been praying for. To the extent it's His work, it will last. But I'm afraid a lot of young people are Jesus People simply because it's popular. They are the ones who will stick only until the next fad comes along, and then it will be good-bye to Jesus.

Now it looked as though the Satan movement was already taking over.

I felt more depressed than ever as other things crowded into my memory. The number of people everywhere I go, talking about horoscopes and astrology. The increasing signs of interest in fortune telling, meditation, Eastern religions, magic, E.S.P., spirits, demons, witchcraft, and Satan himself. The young people, especially, turning to all these things.

Suddenly my thoughts raced back to the days I was leader of the Mau Maus in New York. I thought of Little Bit.

Little Bit was a cute, curly-haired kid about ten years old who kept trying to join the Mau Maus. Everyone in the gang laughed at the idea, of course—the kid was even smaller than his age. We threw him out of our meeting place time after time, but he was always hanging around and he would sneak along behind us when we had a rumble and try to fight on our side.

One night when the Mau Maus were fighting the Bishops, a gang of Phantom Lords showed up behind us. Outnumbered, the Mau Maus had to use an escape route we had reserved for real emergencies. It led over rooftops for a whole block and to get to the last rooftop we had to clear a terrific distance between buildings.

Nighthawk and I were the first across, and everyone in the gang made it to safety. As everyone was rushing down the fire escape, I took a last look back and I saw three Phantom Lords racing across the rooftop behind us—with Little Bit in front of them.

I yelled, "Little Bit! Don't!"

It was too late. Little Bit made a beautiful try. He raced across that roof and sailed across the empty space between the two buildings.

Almost.

He fell just short. His pathetic little hands clawed at the cornice for a moment and then he was gone, and his shriek as he fell ended in a sickening thud in the alley below. No one in the Mau Maus said much about Little Bit after that, but the next time a little kid tried to follow us, we got out our knives, if we had to, to scare him away.

Little Bit was attracted by the thrills of being in a street gang. He had no more idea what he was getting into than the thousands of young people getting sucked into the occult world today.

As I tossed on my bed, my mind shot back to my earliest memories of my boyhood in Puerto Rico. What was it John Ambrose had said about Leif? "He's into reincarnation . . . believing you keep coming back to earth over and over. . . ."

I remembered Mama stirring a big pot of soup in our little kitchen in Las Piedras. "I have not always made soup," she was saying in a dreamy voice. "Once I was a great queen, and many señoritas brought me anything I wished."

I remembered Papa saying something about living many times. For years I had rejected memories like these from my past. They formed a chapter of my life I was glad to leave behind, but now they began to pour back into my consciousness.

While young people today are turning to the glittering attraction of witchcraft, reincarnation, and the whole dark world of the occult as though it were a brand-new toy, I know what it's like. I was born and raised in that world. My own father was a witch, my own mother a medium. I know the appeal of that world—and its incredible dangers.

As I tossed on my bed, a conviction overwhelmed me. I felt as though God were saying:

Nicky, you know the occult world. You have been prepared as no one else to reveal My Light in this darkness. You were not raised up to be silent in such a time as this. You must put what you know into a book.

"Lord," I said silently, "You know I've just signed a contract to do a book about life in the Spirit."

Yes. Write a book about Satan.

I knew God had guided me in signing that contract. I had planned to have a chapter in it on witchcraft, but a whole book about Satan? What would my publishers think if I told them I had an entirely different subject for the book? I had no idea. But the clear impression remained, and I trusted God to clear the way, as He had done so many times before, for His perfect will to be done.

The next morning I shared my thoughts with John Ambrose and his wife.

"Nicky," said John over bacon and eggs, "you know that whenever God does a mighty work, there's an evil backlash. When God sows His good seeds, the devil plants weeds among them. But when the enemy comes in like a flood, the Spirit of the Lord raises up a standard against him. I've often thought that when He led David Wilkerson to give so much of himself to lead you to Christ, He had something bigger in mind for you than anything you've done yet. Maybe the Lord was looking ahead, way back in the 1950s, to what He could do through you twenty years later as evil multiplies. It looks as though He's calling you, Nicky, to the most important assignment I can think of."

Since that day my eyes have been opened as never before to demonic activity—to what I can only call Satan exposing his nakedness. I have been oppressed again and again by evil forces. But at the same time I have become increasingly conscious of the power of God to give peace and deliverance in the midst of evil.

Satan is on the loose! You'll be better-prepared for what he's up to if you'll come with me now to the tropical island where thousands of people used to look to my father and mother for supernatural help.

2

My Father the Witch

From my earliest days I took it for granted that people would come to the door of our stucco house in Las Piedras, Puerto Rico, seeking spirit guidance or healing. But I never paid much attention to the meetings my parents held to get spirit help. The truth is, I never believed in it, and as you probably know from my book *Run Baby Run,* through most of my first fifteen years I was always fighting my father and mother and was only too glad to get away from them.

Soon after I decided I must write this book, I got a telephone call from the Fleming H. Revell Company. "Nicky, we've just finished a staff conference about your book. We think you ought to write a book interpreting the occult scene. We've all been wondering— would you mind holding off the first book while you do this new one?"

"There's nothing I'd rather do!" I said.

To do it, I knew I would have to have some long talks with my mother, who still lives in Las Piedras. My father is gone, but my mother is now a marvelous Christian, active in the Las Piedras Pentecostal church. Whenever I can get a little time for it, I like to drop in on Mama for a good talk. Sometimes I bring her some meat and vegetables and fix her a pot of beef stew while we talk.

I wish you could see Mama. Not many people would believe she was born as early as 1905. There's not a wrinkle on her brow, and her face is filled with peace and love. She is a far-different person from the mother I once almost hated. (And I'm a different son!) When we get together she's likely to preach to me.

"Nicky," Mama will say in Spanish, "how is my boy?"

When I tell her about my youth crusades and the youth outreach centers that keep opening up, Mama will say: "It is good, Nicky. But remember to keep humble. The devil wants to fill you with pride. Remember who put you where you are."

Mama is likely to say, "How is your temper, Nicky?" She remembers what a quick temper I can have. Or she will ask, "How are you getting along with your wife Gloria? You must not let anything come between you. And the granddaughters? You are not spoiling them, are you?"

Mama makes a great Mother Confessor.

But in all the years since she found Christ, Mama had never talked with me about the old days of witchcraft and spiritualism until the summer of 1972. I think we had both been glad to try to forget that chapter in our family life. Now, at last, the time seemed right to talk about it in depth. Soon after my telephone conversation with the publisher I was on a 747 bound for San Juan. I spent as much time as I could in nearby Las Piedras, talking with Mama about witchcraft, spiritualism, and especially about Papa. For what follows here I want to express many thanks to Mama, whose memories helped revive my own about those early days, and the other members of my family I've talked with about my amazing father.

Father was big and strong in both physique and spirit. He was the kind of person who didn't need to raise his voice to command respect; he fairly radiated quiet power. My brothers and I were scared to death when we thought he might find out about something bad we had done, for he was a strict disciplinarian. Yet he was kind as well as firm. We knew that he loved us, and we adored him. Other people did, too, by the hundreds. Papa had an outgoing personality and a great sense of humor. You can get an idea of what people thought of my father from the fact that even though he died in 1964, people still come to our house in Las Piedras looking for him to help them. The Sunday before I visited Mama recently, a tobacco farmer came to our house looking for Papa! Of course Mama talked to him about the Healer who is far greater than "the Great One" of Las Piedras. But when I was small, Jesus Christ was only a name to many people. For practical help, they came to Papa. And when they brought the sick to our house for healing, they were sure that the Great One would do the job.

One man was brought up the hill to our house in a hammock. His leg was so swollen that you might think his hours were numbered. But if you thought that, you didn't know Papa.

"Bring me healing leaves," he said to Mama, who quickly gathered from our garden a great basket of dark green leaves. These Papa spread liberally over the discolored, swollen leg. Then he cupped a vessel of water between his big hands and prayed.

"San Miguel, spirit of strength and life," he said as he seemed to be looking into unfathomable distances, "bind the spirit of evil that attacked my brother. As water cools fire, set apart this water to cool my brother's fever and drive out his sickness."

Now Papa sprinkled the water over the leaf-covered leg. The man groaned and his friends dropped to their knees, moaning and praying.

"When you drink this water," said Papa, "you will be healed."

He lifted the man's head with one hand and held the vessel to his lips with the other. "Drink!" he commanded. "Drink all of it!"

When the man drank, five long things that looked like worms slithered out of his toe, as the swelling began to go down.

Papa's reputation was so great that often there were sick people in hammocks and on stretchers and cots all around our house, brought for the Great One's healing remedies. They came especially for the services on Mondays, Wednesdays and Fridays at the spirit house.

The spirit house, as my brothers and I called it, was a small building with a circular table inside where Mama, Papa, and others gathered for their spirit sessions. Sometimes they met there all day, sometimes in the evenings for several hours, calling on the "good" spirits for help. Father was the president of the spiritualist center of our area. Later the center expanded and a larger spirit house was built nearby.

This new building became a sort of spiritualist theological seminary. When Papa noticed someone with occult powers he brought him to the center for training. One of these trainees, Gomez, is now a spiritualist leader himself. I remember that Gomez once began acting as though he was president of the center. Gomez held a spirit session while Papa was away on a trip to Arecibo. When my father returned, he took Gomez into the spirit house for a meeting between just the two of them and had a long serious talk with him.

As Papa talked, Gomez began to look cold and white and as frightened as anyone I've ever seen. "To do a thing of this kind," Papa said, "it is not enough to have the gifts and the mystic talents. These you have. But unless you learn how to use them properly, you may arouse such powers of destruction as you cannot imagine!"

It was a typically sunny Puerto Rican day, but Papa had barely uttered these words when the sky suddenly became very dark. A flash of lightning shot across the sky and an enormous clap of thunder exploded so loudly that the very ground seemed to shake.

Papa put Gomez under spiritual discipline so effective that in just a short time Gomez came sobbing to Papa, begging his forgiveness. Then Papa put him under a spirit of protection. Gomez learned how dangerous it can be to dabble in occult things.

Early in his psychic career Papa had some dealings in what might be called black magic. One man asked him to put a curse on his enemy. Papa killed a black chicken, sprinkled the blood over the enemy's picture, and then drove a knife through the face. We heard that the man who had been hexed became violently ill.

But Papa turned entirely to white magic and refused to hex anyone after that. "The good spirits must help us drive away the bad spirits," he used to say. "There is no need to deal in destruction. It is better to build up than to tear down."

Papa and Mama believed that the good spirits gave our family protection—but they both had to be on guard against evil spirits. They believed that when they summoned the help of the good

spirits, evil spirits often came with them. So they took every pre-
caution to keep the evil ones away.

When meetings were held at the spirit house, there was usually
a crystal ball or a glass of water in the center of the table. Everyone
at the table concentrated on this while the good spirits were invoked. Mama sat next to Papa, and each person took the hand of
the person next to him until Papa gave permission to let go. Papa
would not do this until he was sure no evil spirits were present. The
ring of hands was believed to keep them out.

One young woman who was brought to the meeting made a deep
impression on everyone who saw her. At times she seemed perfectly normal. At other times wild personalities seemed to take possession of her. Once she pulled up her skirts and made remarks that
made Mama look grim and Papa look embarrassed. Then, suddenly,
her face looked something like an old man's and she was speaking in
an old man's slow, querulous voice, and trembling just the way old
people do. Soon after that she was grinding her teeth and frothing
at the mouth.

The girl was brought to the spirit house and put on a cot there as
the group around the table sought help for her. Suddenly Mama began acting—even looking—almost exactly like the girl. Then the
girl slumped down onto the cot while a trickle of white froth ran
from a corner of Mama's mouth.

Papa ordered everyone to concentrate as he sat intensely still,
his big hand over Mama's. For a long period he sat like a statue,
gazing at Mama as though he could not tear his eyes away. Finally
he relaxed and spoke.

"Aleja," he said, referring to my mother, "has taken this girl's
malady upon herself so that she could help me cure her. Now I know
what to do." (My mother's full name is *Alejandrina,* which can be
translated as Alexandra.)

Papa looked around the building. His gaze came to rest on a
lizard clinging to the wall near a window.

Papa said, "This girl's malady must enter into that lizard. When
it does she will be cured."

All of a sudden the lizard leaped out the window like a shot. The
girl sat up on her cot. Mama straightened up as though she had
just awakened from a long sleep.

My father and mother cooperated in this way to accomplish amazing results. Mama was able to enter into such complete empathy with an afflicted person that she bore that person's sickness or trouble in her own mind and body. When this transfer had been made, Mama opened her mind to the spirits, who told her the real cause of the affliction. Then, often without words, Papa communicated with Mama to learn the cause and remove it. But all this ordinarily happened while Mama was in a state of deep trance, and afterward she usually had no memory of what had happened.

A man who worked on a sugar plantation near Humacao came dragging up the road to our house with listless eyes and a greenish-yellow color to his skin. He said he had been feeling sick for two months and the doctor didn't know what was wrong. During the service Mama began to look so much like this man it was frightening; even her face looked yellowish and drawn. Papa finally told him to dig under the northeast corner of his house.

"You will find seven chicken bones tied to a coffin nail," Papa said. "Burn it all in a fire so hot the iron melts, and the curse that has been laid upon you will be destroyed."

Two days later this man came back leading a goat. He looked 100 percent younger and healthier. He said to Papa: "The bones were there as you said! I followed your instructions and the curse is gone. Please accept this goat as my gift for this miracle."

My father's reputation spread even to the United States. One day a woman came to our house who said she had flown from New York to see Señor Cruz. This woman was very pale and haggard. She said she had met someone from Puerto Rico who told her about my father's power.

"I don't believe in spirits," this American woman told my father, "but I wanted to see what a healer looks like. The Lord knows, no doctor in New York can find out what's wrong with me, and I certainly don't expect you to."

"Sit down," said my father. "I will tell you about yourself."

The woman laughed nervously. "If you can tell very much about me, you must have a good spy system."

"No," said my father. "You do not believe. I will make you believe. I will go to where you came from and describe it to you."

Papa closed his eyes. There was a silence. Then he began to speak slowly. "You do not come from New York, but from a town near New York. You live on a street with many leafy trees. There is an iron fence in front of your house. Someone else lives there with you —two people. Your mother sits in a wheelchair. Your husband walks with a slight limp. He is worried. He is thinking about a very big company that makes telephones and cables. . . ."

Papa stopped speaking because at that moment the visitor turned white and fainted. When she revived, her eyes were wide. "My husband owns a lot of stock in AT&T," she whispered, "and he was talking yesterday about selling some of it. *How could you know?*"

"The spirits show me many things," said Papa. "One thing they show me is why you are ill. A twisted spirit has you in his power. Would you like deliverance?"

Now the woman was sobbing. "I came here to ridicule," she said, "but I will do anything in my power to be well. Please help me!"

Papa stood up and laid his big hands on the woman's head. He closed his eyes. "Twisted one, be gone!"

Again the woman sobbed, this time in joy. "I feel free!" she said. "For the first time in years, I feel free!"

When she left, this woman tried to hand Papa some money but he would not take it. He often refused to take payment for his services. But many people left gifts in gratitude— money, eggs, chickens, pigs, calves, sometimes a goat or even a cow.

Papa told fortunes, too. I suppose he inherited many of his powers from his mother, who used to tell fortunes and heal the sick on the Puerto Rican island of Vieques where Papa was raised. Although she could not read or write, Señora Cruz would tell expectant mothers what kind of babies they would have, and she was more accurate than the doctors or nurses in predicting the time of birth.

I cannot doubt that my father had psychic powers. But neither can I forget two other things about him.

Sometimes Papa would become possessed by a spirit he could not control. I remember once he grabbed my youngest brother, put a rope around his neck, and started to hang him from the limb of a tree. It took the combined fury of Mama and my brothers and me to bring Papa back to his senses and save the boy Papa and Mama dearly loved—when they were themselves—from strangulation.

And there was one person Papa could not help. Before he met my mother, he had married and become father of three children on the island of Vieques. His son Angelin sometimes acted very strangely. Once he ran away from home and was found by farmers on the other side of the island—completely naked, babbling, and fighting like a wild animal. Sometimes Angelin beat his head so hard against a wall, and became so wild that Papa had to tie him up.

Papa himself had had fits like that in his teens. It was this, in fact, that helped steer Papa into witchcraft. When Papa was about seventeen he believed he had learned how to control the spirit that used to come over him and make him act like a madman. Through his seventy-eight years he delivered many sufferers from a similar malady—but nothing he did helped Angelin.

Then one day Angelin went into a revival service in a little Pentecostal church. When the invitation was given he went forward and knelt down—and was delivered completely from his inexplicable problem. Today Angelin is a happy Christian. Looking at him, you would never think he had once been subject to these strange fits. *Jesus brought Angelin the complete healing that in this case Papa couldn't deliver.*

Papa had some strong medicine, but Mama found some that was even stronger.

3

My Mother the Medium

Anyone who sees my mother now, with her bright black eyes and serene face framed in white hair, would hardly guess that for most of her life she was deeply involved in the occult.

In the late 1920s my mother was the lovely Señorita Alejandrina Velasquez. Like my father, she seemed to have a natural gift for psychic things, and from her teens she was active in spiritualistic meetings in San Juan. When Galo Cruz came to that city from Vieques, the beautiful, young medium and the rugged man of Vieques were drawn to each other. Soon after their marriage they set up the spiritualist center in Las Piedras where they spent so many years.

Mama was a marvelous co-worker with Papa. As I have mentioned, she often permitted the afflictions of those who came to us for help to enter her own body, so that she and Papa might learn the cause and seek the cure.

It was not pleasant or easy, however, to bear the sufferings of those who came to the center. And it wasn't always certain what might happen. Once when Papa and Mama were treating a patient in the spirit house, a spirit came upon Mama with such force that she was catapulted clear over the table. Sometimes she was possessed with such a furious presence that it took many men and women to hold her. And my mother is not a large or muscular person.

Some people would call my mother a sensitive, or a natural psychic, or a woman gifted with extrasensory powers. All this she probably is and was, like my father and many of my fellow Puerto Ricans. There may well be more powers in the human mind than anyone has yet begun to explore. And some people, like my parents, may be unusually gifted in this area. During my boyhood, however, everyone I knew took it for granted that Mama and Papa did their work through the help of deceased spirits.

Sometimes people would come to our house asking Mama to get in touch with a dead member of the family. Then, occasionally in our living room but usually in the big spirit house, everyone would sit in a circle and wait for the spirit to reveal its presence. Sometimes this would be through Mama or Papa, sometimes through another medium. But just as Papa was known throughout our island as El Taumaturgo, the Wonder Worker, and as the Witch and the Great One, Mama was known as the Medium.

Going back to what I just said about the powers of the mind, you are probably wondering if I believe Mama really contacted the spirits of the dead. I don't—but neither can I believe she simply drew on psychic or telepathic power. I'm convinced it's a lot more complicated than that. But let me come back to this subject later.

Once when my parents were celebrating a seance in our home with some other mediums, my little brother Rafi, who was then about six years old, came into the room and sidled up to Mama. Suddenly she shot out her hands and held him so tightly around the neck that he began to scream, "Mama, what's wrong with you?"

Mother remembers it this way:

"I couldn't understand what Rafi was saying. Another identity had taken complete control of my mind and body. My husband looked at me and ordered the spirit to leave me. When it left, I felt weak and exhausted; I could not remember anything that had happened."

Of course this murderous impulse was completely uncharacteristic of Mama, for both she and Papa deeply loved Rafi.

Sometimes Mama would spread out a pack of tarot cards while

she looked at one of us children, and we knew she was looking at our future lives. But she didn't need cards to tell many things about a person. After one woman in Las Piedras dropped in for a visit, Mama said matter-of-factly, "She will die soon." The next day the woman was struck by a careening car that ran up onto the sidewalk where she was standing, and died on the way to the hospital. But the cards gave Mama a complete picture of a person's future. However, she never talked to any of us eighteen children about what she had learned. She must have realized that some things are best left with God.

Soon after Mama and Papa moved into their new home in Las Piedras, Mama saw the Great Depression coming. She had a vision of many acres of ground burned over, and she saw the economic destruction coming. Mama advised the people who came to our house to start saving for hard times, and in the bleak days of the 1930s many of them remembered her warnings.

On January 6, 1940, a spirit visited Mama in the night. It told her that Japan would attack the United States and that a great war would reach deep into Puerto Rico; every male between the ages of eighteen and forty-five, it predicted, would soon be drafted. If Mama had read or listened to the news, she might not have believed what she was told, for at that time nothing seemed farther from probability than an attack against the United States by Japan, a country considered too tiny and backward for the military experts to pay it much attention. But almost exactly two years later, the sneak attack of December 7, 1941, bringing America into World War II, confirmed the accuracy of Mama's revelation. The fact is that while Mama was well-educated by Puerto Rican standards, she never paid any more attention to the radio or newspapers than Papa. They were both so deeply involved in their family and their work that they had little time for the news. Anyway, they got the important news in advance!

My mother has never known any English, but one time I came home from school a few minutes behind my brother Salvador, and I found him shaking with laughter. "Listen to Mama!" he whispered.

Mama was in our living room saying something that sounded like jabbering at first, but I caught on as Salvador translated. We had been studying English in school, and now Mama was speaking that language in a voice that sounded exactly like a cultured Englishman's. I don't remember now what she said; I do remember that Salvador was so amazed by the whole thing that he suddenly turned white and fainted, and at first my father thought that a spirit had taken possession of Salvador, too.

When Mama came out of her trance, Salvador asked her in English: "Hello, Mother. What is for supper?"

Mama looked at him blankly, then burst out in Spanish: "Why don't you speak so I can understand you?"

She had no idea that she had just been speaking English.

Mama was a good mother and must have been a tremendous help to Papa. Anyone looking at them could see how much they loved each other. Mama was always relaxed and happy-looking when she was with Papa.

I have already told you that Mama is now a Christian. You are probably waiting for me to say that she once lived in fear and despair, and now she knows perpetual peace and joy.

It isn't quite like that.

My mother was never afraid until she became a Christian.

Mama and Papa did their best to raise their eighteen children to be good and do good. (There are only fourteen of us now; four of my brothers have died over the years.) And in general my parents succeeded remarkably well. My sister Carmen and my brothers studied hard, married fine partners, and are raising their children to be like themselves — stalwart, conscientious individuals. They love their children and to a high degree are living up to my parents' dreams for them. Two of my brothers are now teachers in Puerto Rico; one is a minister in New York City.

The first time they got word I had been arrested after I came to New York, Mama and Papa were deeply distressed. Papa made several trips to New York to try to straighten me out.

Early in 1958 Papa visited me in jail. He brought with him a message from Mama.

"Nicky," he said, "Mama asked me to tell you that you are breaking our hearts. She said, 'Tell him he is killing me. Tell him this:

'Surely a bad spirit has got hold of you, Nicky. Get rid of it before it is too late.' Maybe this will be the last time I ever see you, Nicky. Maybe you will never see Mama again. Change your ways now, while you still have a chance."

I couldn't do that, of course – not by myself. Even the psychiatrist who had been appointed to help me finally gave up on me. But that very year God used David Wilkerson to change Nicky Cruz into a new creature.

I wrote my parents about this unbelievable thing that had happened to me.

Slowly Papa began to change. Now he dealt with the spirits less and less; before he died he had stopped his occult dealings entirely.

Mama had many painful moments. She had always tried to lead a good life, and at first it didn't make sense to her that the black sheep in the family – me – *Nicky* – had changed his color and wanted to lead the rest of the family to God. She had often asked herself where she had failed with me; I am sure she felt that somehow she had started me on the road to degradation. Her heart was torn and troubled as she searched her conscience, but there was no peace for many months.

Mama had many questions about Jesus. To her he had always been a good spirit, and there was no question that she had always believed in God according to her light. So had Papa. Nominally they were Catholics, although they only went to mass once or twice a year. (They took us children when we were small but at a very early age I decided mass was a lot of nonsense and stopped going.)

Of course there were Protestants in Las Piedras. But our family had less use for them than for the Catholic church. Papa used to say that the Pentecostals were crazy fanatics and the Evangelicals were dead. "I have more power than they have," he once chuckled. So Mama struggled all by herself with the new ideas that came to her from my letters. My brother Frank wrote her, too, about the change in my life.

After I had had two years of Bible training in La Puente, California, with my third and last year still ahead of me, I flew back to Puerto Rico to talk personally with my family and friends. One night my mother and two of my brothers accepted Jesus as their Saviour and Lord.

This was the beginning of some wonderful things. Before long three of my brothers were in Bible institutes. My brother Frank became a missionary-evangelist in Colombia, Guatemala, and other parts of South America, and is today a pastor in Brooklyn, New York.

For Mama it was the beginning of a new kind of life. There was a dimension to it now that she had never dreamed of before. She began praying for two hours a day, not because anyone told her she had to, but because she wanted to be alone with her new-found Shepherd as much as possible, and because there were so many things to talk over with him.

One night great flames lit the sky on our hilltop in Las Piedras. Neighbors rushing up the street from the village to help my family fight the fire were startled to see Mama standing in our driveway with her arms folded while the two spirit houses crackled in flame.

"I set fire to them myself," Mama told the incredulous spectators. "There will be no more spirit seances at the Witch's House. We will worship only one spirit now—the Holy Spirit."

But being a Christian isn't simple and effortless for anyone. Those genuinely committed to Christ face a constant struggle—and for those who were once involved in the occult, the struggle is multiplied many times.

The spirits Mama renounced have not given her up. They are always after her.

Many of Mama's former spiritualist friends, of course, are bitterly opposed to her Christian stand. They see it as an attack on what they are doing, and of course it is. So they attack back—and my mother faces hostility from that direction.

In her Las Piedras church Mother finds fellowship and strength. But there has been deep division and bitterness there too. Some heartrending events in the congregation have resulted in the expulsion of two people close to Mother's heart. Surely Satan has been at work, even within the church.

Satan always attacks, of course, at our weakest points. With my father at her side, Mother never had to be afraid. Now, old and alone, she is subjected to frightening incidents.

Just two weeks before I visited Mother in the summer of 1972, one of my brothers came to her house at 1:30 A.M. and knocked in the special way he has to let her know who it was. She opened the door and let him stay for the night, as he sometimes does.

At 4:30 A.M. Mother was awakened by exactly the same steps on the porch, exactly the same pattern of knocking as before. She went to the door and no one was there.

Things like this have often happened to my mother since she became a Christian. She is more afraid than the average woman would be, for she knows the malevolent power behind the strange noises and inexplicable events that come to her. But she also knows the Saviour who guards her with His own omnipotence.

"Once I lived in peace," Mama said to me recently, "because the devil was sure I was his. Now that I have come out of the darkness into the light, he is like an angry lion. His demons are always around me, but so are Christ's angels, and Christ is stronger than all the demons."

Yes, frightening things have happened to my mother since she met Christ, but much more frightening ones happened to my father.

4

One Prize the Devil Didn't Win

When they were in witchcraft my father and mother never dreamed that they were being used by evil spirits. They sincerely *thought* they were helping people through the aid of good spirits.

They know the truth now.

Father was so deeply under spirit subjection that he spent nearly eighty years without Christ. The truth came to him the minute he made a move toward the Saviour I found in 1958 in New York.

Before he died, Father told me of the torture that began when he first seriously considered joining Mother and me in a clear-cut decision to enthrone Jesus Christ as Lord and Saviour. "It has been torture, Nicky," he said from his white hospital bed. "The spirits came to me from the north and the south, the east and the west. They told me they would take away all my power and protection. They said they would kill me the instant I publicly came out for Christ. They threatened to torture and kill every member of my family.

"I know their power, Nicky," Father sobbed. "I have given my life to what I thought was a good thing. Now I see clearly they were lying and deceiving."

"There is no power like God's, Father," I said.

"I know it, Nicky. You have proved it in your life. But spirit power—that is real too, Nicky. I want to be a Christian, my son, but I don't dare."

I wished I could stay in Las Piedras and give Satan the biggest rumble of my life. How I would have liked to battle him for my father's soul! But God was calling me to other work, and I do not underestimate the power and cunning of man's oldest adversary. I would not have dared to touch my father without a clear indication from above. I cannot think of anything more dangerous than dealing with evil spirits. There are cases that yield to nothing but prayer and fasting, as Jesus taught us, and at that time I did not have the time nor the command to win my father's soul from the enemy. That work was to be done by others.

About four years before he died, Father was taken with a malady the doctors did not understand. While he went in and out of the hospital during those years, Father drew great strength from a man named Choco Davila.

Choco was a thoroughly-Christian businessman. Weekdays he ran his business, supplying materials for various construction projects. Saturdays, Sundays, evenings, and as often as possible on the job, Choco Davila worked for the Lord.

Choco was an outstanding member of his church. When it was testimony time, he was rarely without an expression of thankfulness for what God had done for him. When the pastor was away, Choco often filled the pulpit. And what sermons he preached! While my father had little use for most sermons and preachers, he loved the messages Choco gave. So he often went to hear Choco speak.

Choco Davila was a far cry from the hellfire-and-damnation preachers who sometimes fill our Puerto Rican pulpits. Father liked him because what he said was always intelligent and logical and never condemnatory. Yet he preached the message of the Bible. From Choco's sermons it was clear that spiritualism is definitely not a way to heaven, but Choco never denounced spiritualism. He just explained what the Bible said, so clearly and attractively that it was hard not to agree.

Choco Davila visited our home many times during Father's last years. On one of his first visits, he read the Bible and talked—and

Father wept. Then Choco put his hands on Father's head and began to pray.

Father was sitting in a rocking chair in our living room at that time. Underneath the rocker slept his dog, Diablo. As Choco laid his hands on Father's head, Diablo leapt up with a growl like a lion roaring and charged with such fury that Choco ran from the house. Choco promised to come back, and did, but Father said: "When anything good comes into my life, something like this always happens."

Mother read the Bible to Father during those last years. On one occasion, as she read, both she and Father saw tongues of fire leaping up from the pages. Father had never read the second chapter of Acts, I'm sure, nor ever talked about tongues of fire. But he knew a miraculous sign when he saw one. From that moment he was convinced what he must do.

The last time Father was in the hospital, many mediums came to visit him and many other people tried to get in to seek his help as they had done in the past. (Mother kept as many of these people away as she could.) There were also many Christians who came to see him.

I had a wonderful talk with Father in the hospital. He said: "My son, I want Christ. The spirits keep coming to me, threatening me with what they will do to me and to all of you if I ask Christ to come in. I am still afraid of them, Nicky. But my choice is made. I am going to give my life to Jesus, Nicky. When I do this, I will ask Him to take me then."

Soon after that Father returned to our home and I had to return to the United States. Father asked Mother to invite Choco Davila to come in again, and he spoke simply but eloquently of the old, old story of Jesus and His love. He read to Father from the third chapter of John and the eighth chapter of Romans. When he prayed for Father, Father gripped Choco's hand. Then he called Mother.

"Aleja," said Father to my mother with a tremendous light in his face. "I have done it! Jesus is mine! *Gloria a Dios!* Alleluia!"

Eight hours later Father died. Jesus took him home as he had asked, and the devil lost a prize at the very gates of death.

More than seven thousand people came to my father's funeral in

Las Piedras. It was the biggest funeral the village ever had. My sister and brothers and I cried like babies when he was buried, and we were not the only ones.

I have often thought what a tremendous Christian my father would have made if he had come to Christ earlier. He had such tremendous gifts and insight — he could spot a phony a mile off, and he gave of himself the best way he knew. Well, now he has all eternity to serve his Saviour. May his life speak, too, through this memory of a man who was truly a Great One.

5

Satan's Son

By now you probably know that I believe there are such things as evil spirits, and that under their leader, Satan, they can do awful things to human beings. I believe this with all my heart because I have had my own dealings with the spirit world.

When my mother called me "Satan's son" during a spiritualistic trance in 1948, how close to the truth was she? Certainly I gave my parents, my teachers — almost everyone who knew me — a very hard time.

During my first eighteen years it often seemed like two beings were struggling with each other deep inside me. Part of me loved my strong father and my lovely mother and my sister Carmen and all sixteen of my brothers — how proud of them I felt, sometimes, when we were all together! But another part of me came to hate them so much that I was almost happy when I had the chance to fly to New York and leave them far behind. Part of me wanted to do what was right — and part of me hated authority and goodness.

They talk about mixed-up kids, but I was more mixed up than anyone I can think of. As a rule my brothers liked school, learned fast, were gentle and polite, a lot like my parents. I was the odd one. I hated school and my teachers. I loved practical jokes. I grated against people like sandpaper.

Once when I was little I threw a rock down our hill and it bounced off the ground by a mango tree and knocked over a little girl, Maria, who was playing there in her yard with her sister. I ducked out of sight and no one knew who threw the rock. Maria was bleeding and was unconscious for a while. I had the funniest feeling when I heard people talking about her. I was scared, but something inside me felt excited and satisfied when I thought maybe I'd killed her.

I used to steal from Mama. Papa caught me at it once. After that I always watched to see that no one was around when I took coins or bills out of the basket where Mama thought nobody knew she kept them. I never took enough at one time so she would notice it, and I got a big thrill out of fooling her and outwitting Papa that way.

As I got bigger I stole more — sometimes several dollars a day. One time I bought a watch with this easily acquired money, another time a BB gun. With this I liked to hide where no one could see me and pepper the legs of unsuspecting passersby. Of course, I kept such things as the watch and gun hidden away from the sight of Mama and Papa. I knew I'd get a punishment I'd not soon forget if they ever found out what I was doing.

Sometimes I would steal a dime or a quarter and buy a ticket to the movie theatre in Las Piedras. I loved to watch Tarzan of the Apes swinging through far-off jungles that reminded me of our own rain forest a few miles away. And I was especially fond of cowboy heroes — Roy Rogers, the Lone Ranger, and El Lobo, the Latin outlaw who could always outwit his enemies with a fast horse and a good gun.

One of the things I bought with the money I stole was a bicycle. That really made me somebody. I kept it away from our house, and when Mama and Papa learned I had a bicycle, I invented a long story about how another boy had loaned it to me, and they believed me.

With my bike I could do all kinds of things. One day I was coasting along a dirt road between Las Piedras and Melelitas when I passed a little kid carrying two bottles of Coke. I reached down and snatched one bottle away from him. This little boy spun around to see what was happening, stubbed his toe, and dropped the other bottle on a rock. As I went around a bend in the road I could see this kid standing there crying, and that sight made me feel even better than getting a free Coke. I could picture how he felt, and the licking he would probably get when he got home with no money and no Coke. Now it hurts me to think of it, but then it made me laugh with glee.

When I got to New York I really dug the gang life. Every time my fist thudded against a skull, I got a tremendous charge out of that contact. And when we were fighting with knives, it felt good to rip a knife through skin and see blood spurt out and feel the blade grate against the bone.

Every so often some different thing comes back to me from those days of the gangs, and I wonder how I could have been the way I was. Like the night Nighthawk and Mingo and I were trying out a car we stole off the streets and drove past a guy we recognized as Little George, a member of the Forty-Niners. That was a small gang that had caught two Mau Maus three days before and burned their faces with acid.

Nighthawk was driving. He slammed on the brakes and Mingo and I jumped out and shoved Little George into the car before he knew what was happening. We held him and used our knives and cigarettes for a while to make him jump and yell, while Nighthawk drove all over the deserted streets of Brooklyn and Harlem.

At last we decided to dump Little George. Nighthawk was hitting about sixty-five on the Harlem River Drive when Mingo opened the door and we pushed Little George out so he bounced off a concrete abutment.

Now it makes me sick to think about it. But while we were doing things like that, it was more a thrill than anything else. I felt revved-up and filled-full as though I'd just had a big meal or a girl, and we sang songs all the way home.

Many times before I became a Christian I was conscious of a tremendous force that had me in its control. Somehow I knew that what I was doing was part of a design and a purpose greater than my own—a design and purpose bent on evil and destruction. At such times I was in the grip of a terrible fear.

On one of these occasions I almost killed my brother Gene. Gene is a wonderful fellow. He's only a year older than me, and when he

invited me to stay with him for awhile we were very close. He was
a real Big Brother to me. He had a good job and he had given me
some money and taken me shopping with him at Macy's and
Ohrbach's in Manhattan. We had a great time going through all the
departments, watching the girls going up the escalators, and getting
so many things that we left most of them to be delivered to Gene's
apartment. I remember I got two new pairs of shoes and a sharp
jacket and Gene bought a necklace for his girl friend, Lucia.

On the subway back I kidded Gene about the necklace. "You
give her too much," I said. "Girls are for kicks. What's the good of
giving them all these things? Love 'em and split is my philosophy."

I was partly kidding, but more than half serious. The truth is, I
resented the way Gene lived. He was always courteous, polite,
and bright in school, and he treated girls like they would break if
you handled them rough. I didn't, and it made me mad that he did.

"Lucia will like this," said Gene, patting the pocket where he had
put the necklace.

"I can think of girls who would give you more than she will—
cheaper!" I said.

Gene changed the subject, and nothing much happened until we
got to Broadway and Lafayette, where we had to change subway
trains and catch the *D* train back to Brooklyn.

It seemed like a long wait as we stood by the tracks waiting for
the *D* train to arrive. I wasn't thinking about anything in particular
when the lights came around a bend in the subway tunnel.

Suddenly the most overwhelming feeling came over me, an impulse to push Gene in front of the train that came charging down
the tunnel toward us. It was a feeling of evil, of anger, of hate—
pure and simple. The horrible thought took possession of my mind:

*The subway needs a victim. Your brother is to be victim. Offer
the sacrifice NOW before the moment is gone!*

I could picture myself pushing Gene in front of the train, the roaring cars, the flashing wheels, the mangled body, the flying blood.
Gene—with his moral superiority—gone from my life!

He is standing there waiting. NOW!

I moved toward him. His back was turned to me, oblivious. I
felt that the one thing I had to do was push him over the edge of the

subway platform, watch his body hurtle beneath the grinding wheels, get rid of him forever. The feeling was a blinding, driving force inside me. My hands shot out like pistons.

But there was a spark of warmth in my heart that was not quite out. This was *my brother,* who had always been so good and generous to me!

"Gene!" I screamed.

Gene whirled around, leaped to one side as I fought to keep my body from doing what my brain had been commanding. Alarm filled his face as he saw mine. My thoughts must have been written in my eyes, for he turned white.

"Nicky!" he gasped. "What's the matter? What are you doing?"

The *D* train opened its doors, let out its passengers, shut its doors again, and took off into the darkness as we stood there looking at each other.

"I don't know," I said. "Something must have come over me."

Gene's face crumpled up and he began to cry as he realized what I had nearly done. "Oh, Nicky!" he sobbed. "What is wrong with you?"

I didn't know—except that I had nearly lost control of everything decent and human that was left inside of me.

Another time I was in the subway station near Prospect Park, waiting for a train that seemed to take forever to arrive. As I stood there leaning against the dirty wall, the most awful wave of loneliness and emptiness swept over me. I thought of all the mean things I had done, of my home far away, of the future—*what* future? Would I end up like the Mau Mau who had been buried recently, killed in a gang war, or in Sing Sing? What was the point to life, anyway? Was I cursed to be Satan's son forever?

My thoughts turned from the abstract to the concrete. Why was the stupid subway train so late? Why did everything always turn out wrong?

All of a sudden, I smelled something burning. I felt something warm—hot—on my hip. I looked down and saw smoke coming out of my pocket. I slapped it, burned my hand and hip, emptied my pocket of the paper of matches that had burst into flame.

How? I hadn't been smoking. There was no earthly reason for those matches to ignite — but they had caught fire. My mind flashed back to the strange things my parents had sometimes done in Puerto Rico. *No connection,* I told myself, but I couldn't deny all that I had seen as a youngster. Was this strange fire a reminder that I was Satan's son?

I could never explain why those matches caught fire. I still can't. I don't know how Daniel Home of Scotland once stirred the burning embers in a fireplace with his face, or could hold a red-hot coal in his hand without being burned, or how Indian fakirs can walk through fire. I don't know how Nelya Mikhailova of Leningrad can make a heavy bottle move across a shelf, as she concentrates, and crash to the floor. Competent witnesses testify that these things happen.

Many times when I was in my room in Brooklyn I felt angry, desperately lonely, depressed. While part of me gloated over my life of crime and rebellion, part felt guilty and sad and hopeless, and I heard again and again the sound of my mother's voice: *Son of Satan, child of devil! Mark of beast on his heart! Hand of Lucifer on his life!*

At such times I often felt like selling out completely to the devil. I had come close to it. I think now that there is a point in anyone's life that, once crossed, it is humanly speaking impossible to go back. At those times I was desperately close to that line. I could practically hear a sinister voice saying:

Give up. Let me take over. I promise you more fun than you can dream of. Why don't you quit fighting and let me take control?

I'm stubborn. I guess I was 99 percent Satan's, but I still held on to a few shreds of decency and self-respect. I wasn't willing to give myself over completely to anyone.

(I could also sense, from little things they hinted at, that many of the guys in the Mau Maus were feeling the same kind of struggle. We lived so close to hell all the time, it's a wonder any of us escaped total destruction. But bad as we were, some of us held out against giving in completely to the Evil One.)

So when I got depressed I would often puff on sticks of marijuana until I had drowned out reality and drifted into troubled dreams. Sometimes I'd knock myself out with wine or rum. And sometimes when nothing else worked I got so desperate I pounded the wall with my fists until my knuckles bled, or banged my head against the wall until I was unconscious. I was like a caged animal, desperate to get out but not knowing how. I felt evil and guilty and helpless.

Still, I was proud and stubborn. I knew I was going straight down-hill fast, but I wasn't willing or able to turn around.

I guess that pride and stubbornness was one reason I hated David Wilkerson so when I first saw him. Here was a guy who seemed *completely* dominated by a Spirit absolutely the opposite of nearly everything I held to—and he wanted me to be dominated by the same Spirit! I wanted Nicky Cruz to be in the saddle first and last.

When I did give in to the Holy Spirit, as you probably know, the floodgates of my soul burst open. The springs of love and emotion that had nearly dried up, burst into life like an oil gusher shooting up through a desert. The conflict and the loneliness and guilt were replaced with the most incredible sense of peace and forgiveness and bubbling, irrepressible joy. Nicky Cruz was born all over again into a completely new creature!

But Satan has more tricks up his sleeve than anyone would believe possible.

6

Who Is Stronger?

While I was writing this book a friend told me of a conversation the Reverend W. Elwyn Davies, a mission director in Toronto, had with a college girl. Dr. Davies had been speaking at a Christian retreat, and after the meeting this girl came to him and asked him:

"Which is stronger, Christ or Satan?"

"What do you mean?" Dr. Davies countered. "Jesus Christ has all power in heaven and earth. Don't you believe that?"

"Yes," said the girl, "I believe that. But you don't understand. I mean—*which is really stronger, Christ or Satan?*"

Then the girl explained why she had asked this strange-sounding question. She said that when she was quite young she and some neighbor children had started playing with a Ouija board. It all started as a simple children's game, but before long the children seemed to be in contact with a strange entity that fascinated them with answers to questions that led them deeper and deeper into a bizarre new world. The upshot of it was that the young people made a pact with the devil.

Through the Inter-Varsity Fellowship at her college this girl was led to Christ. But Satan would not let her alone. He surrounded her with so many strange events and temptations that she became frightened that he would yet get her back into his power. So she really wondered: "Which is stronger?"

Dr. Davies talked with the girl for a long time. Finally they prayed and separated. When Dr. Davies got up to go on his way, he discovered he was so weak that he had to drink a whole bottle of Coca-Cola before he had enough energy to walk away.

Dr. Davies did not see that college girl again, but at another meeting in another city he was approached by a young lady who said, "Do you know _____?" She named the girl Dr. Davies had talked with about Christ and Satan. When he said that he did, she said: "She asked me to tell you something I hope you understand better than I do. She said, 'If you see the Reverend Davies, tell him that now I know Christ is stronger.' "

Anyone who has ever been close to Satan knows how strong and relentlessly persistent he can be. I wish I could say that when I accepted Christ, or even when I was baptized by the Holy Spirit, everything was sunshine and joy.

It just isn't so.

Since I found God, I have had some wonderful times with Him. I have also had some experiences when the devil drew so close, I shudder to remember it.

Once when I was holding a youth crusade in a southern city, Gloria and I stayed in a rooming house owned by a Reverend Smith. Reverend Smith was pastor of a large church and had quite a reputation for his work with children and young people. He was always having conferences and camps and retreats for these youngsters, and seemed like a pleasant-enough man; certainly he was a successful, hard-working minister.

But there was something about this man that repelled me. And something about the house that smelled of evil. I couldn't put my finger on it at the time, although I sensed something wrong.

I had some great times telling the young people about Christ and winning some of them for the Lord. It was heady work. I found that it drove me to my knees, to Scripture and prayer and times of fasting, as the power of God began to work through me.

Then came an experience that is still hard for me to understand. Never before have I mentioned this except to a few close friends, for reasons that will be apparent. One night, Gloria and I went to a

downtown mission in the city with a number of the personal workers
and ministers supporting the crusade. We played and sang and witnessed — I'm no musician but I'm never bashful telling what God
has done for me — and half a dozen men and a half-drunk woman
came to the altar in response. It was a thrilling time for a guy who
used to look at drunks mainly as easy people to rob.

That night as Gloria slept I tossed and turned. The sense of evil
was there in the house. You may not believe that evil can permeate
a specific place or person, but I have experienced it many times. I
am aware when a man or woman is filled with the Spirit of God and
when it's just a put-on. I have seen many drug addicts that I know
were possessed by Satan. I know when the devil walks into a room.
That night I felt him in mine.

Gloria turned in her sleep and the street light fell across her lovely
throat.

An obscene impulse came into my mind.

Choke her, it urged.

The thought was so contrary to anything I could imagine, I was
appalled. I jumped out of bed and got on my knees.

"Lord," I cried out, "help me! You know how I love Gloria.
Help me get rid of this awful thought. Help me!"

Something slimy and indecent said, *Choke her.*

I rushed over to Gloria's side of the bed. "Wake up, Gloria!" I
cried as I grabbed her hand. "Wake up! I need you!"

"I'm too tired, Nicky," Gloria said, as she started to turn over.

"No, Gloria! It isn't what you think. Wake up!" I shook her a
little. "Gloria, you've got to help me. The devil is here. Get up —
please — and help me pray."

I prayed again. I reminded God of His promises to defend us
against evil. I told Him there was only one thing I wanted, to love
and serve Him, but I needed His help right then mighty bad. I
pleaded with Him to help me overcome the power of Satan.

Then Gloria prayed. She didn't say as much as I did, but as she
talked to Jesus I felt His power beginning to cover me like a
shield.

"Gloria," I said, "I've just had a terrible temptation. It's too awful to even tell you about now. Lay your hands on me, Gloria, and plead the blood of Jesus against the devil."

Gloria laid her cool, firm hands on my head and made the most wonderful prayer. I felt the strength of the Holy Spirit flow into me, and when she had finished, I knew that the tempter had gone.

When we had got back into bed, Gloria pressed my hand. "What happened, Nicky?" she asked.

I told her. I told her the whole impossible story as truthfully and completely as I knew how. You can get an idea of what a great Christian and great person Gloria is when I say that she has never let that experience make the slightest rift between us.

Later some of the parents in Reverend Smith's church started asking him some questions about his conduct with the young people that led to an official inquiry. After an investigation, he was defrocked for homosexual molestation.

Another time when Satan drew very close to me was when I was working at Teen Challenge in New York. In the first flush of my enthusiasm at being a co-worker with David Wilkerson I worked day and night. I led groups into the worst sections of New York. I went to Spanish Harlem, Black Harlem, and the Bronx. I prayed for three hours a day and fasted for two days a week. I worked so hard and fasted so much I got as skinny as a rail.

Amazing things happened. One day we brought in ten heroin addicts. Many of the addicts were delivered and transformed in miraculous ways.

During this period a cab pulled up in front of the white building at 416 Clinton Avenue. Out of it crawled one of the most pathetic looking creatures I've ever seen. Shaking like a leaf, this white-faced young man handed the cabbie what was probably his last dollar and wavered into the building.

"Someone said you help addicts," he said to the girl at the receptionist's desk. "Do you think you can do anything for me?"

"I can't," said the girl, "but God can. What is your name?"

"Luis Rosario."

Luis had been on drugs for eight years. I have never seen anyone more fidgety and restless. We gave him the usual treatment – prayer, prayer, and more prayer. Luis took to it like a starving dog to a platter of raw meat. He let the Spirit of the living God fill him completely.

Luis went on to the La Puente Bible Institute and for a while worked with the Teen Challenge centers in Puerto Rico. Today he and his very capable wife, Carmen, direct the Alcance Juvenil, our youth outreach center just outside San Juan. I can't think of anyone I would rather have in charge of this important work. Luis is a strong, confident, radiant Christian, steady as a rock – the kind of man you would trust with anything. He and Carmen are carrying out a tremendous ministry.

That was the kind of transformation that was continually taking place those days at the Teen Challenge Center in Brooklyn where Gloria and I were working – which makes it so hard to understand what happened in the midst of that powerful evidence of the working of God.

An evil spirit came to the center.

Many of us felt it. When we gathered in the prayer room, there was a note of special urgency in the petitions. "Deliver us from evil" became our constant request.

One night when I got to our room, where Gloria was already asleep, I hadn't taken two steps into the room when I felt strongly that something was wrong. I tiptoed into the room next to ours and sat down on an empty cot. Fear chilled my stomach. I felt as weak as a baby.

A horrible command flashed across my consciousness.

Kill Gloria.

"No!" I almost shrieked. "Jesus – where are You?"

I wondered if I was going insane. I felt so weak I held on to the mattress. The room circled around me. What was happening?

A spirit of destruction hung like a heavy fog in the air. I did not know until later that at the same time one of my staff members, Larry White, felt the same sense of impending destruction, of an evil, murderous attack. He got out of his bed and began to pray.

I went back to our room to warn Gloria. When her eyes fluttered open as I put my hand on her shoulder, I said, "Wake up, Gloria. Something is wrong. I'm losing my mind, pray for me!"

Gloria came awake and reached for her Bible. "Let me read you a Psalm," she said.

This was one time I didn't want the Bible read. "There's no time for that, Gloria. Don't do anything right now but pray! Somebody wants to destroy us. Pray!"

For forty-five minutes Gloria and I prayed. Then, relieved a little, I told Gloria to go back to bed while I went downstairs to the prayer room to pray some more.

I found five other Teen Challenge workers already there. They too had felt the evil presence and were seeking the only defense there is.

"Jesus," I implored, "kick the devil out of here!"

We said it many different ways, but that was the thing we all asked for. And God answered. The spirit of oppression lifted and we went back the next day to snatching souls from the Evil One.

I thought about those two incidents many times. If I had told a psychiatrist about them, I have no doubt that he would have labeled me a murderous psychotic. I'm no psychiatrist, but I know just enough about such things to realize that I had been twice in a very dangerous condition. Was my mind going? Was the power of Satan too much for me? Why had I let those murderous impulses into my mind?

Why *Gloria*—of all people? God knows how much she means to me. He picked her out of all the girls on earth just for me, and many is the time she and her influence have kept me from wrong. If I were to tell you what Gloria means to me, I would have to quote the closing words of Proverbs:

> Who can find a virtuous woman? for her price is far above rubies.
> The heart of her husband doth safely trust in her, so that he shall have no need of spoil.
> She will do him good and not evil all the days of her life.

She seeketh wool, and flax, and worketh willingly with
her hands.

She is like the merchants' ships; she bringeth her food
from afar.

She riseth also while it is yet night, and giveth meat to
her household, and a portion to her maidens.

Strength and honour are her clothing; and she shall re-
joice in time to come.

She openeth her mouth with wisdom: and in her tongue
is the law of kindness.

She looketh well to the ways of her household, and
eateth not the bread of idleness.

Her children arise up, and call her blessed; her husband also, and he praiseth her.

Many daughters have done virtuously, but thou excel-
lest them all.

Favour is deceitful, and beauty is vain: but a woman
that feareth the LORD, she shall be praised.

Give her of the fruit of her hands; and let her own
works praise her in the gates.

                                        Proverbs 31:10–15, 25–31

Everyone needs someone to go to with questions like the ones
that wracked my heart and mind after those two experiences with
Satan. I was blessed in finding at the Bible institute in La Puente a
man you could ask questions like that and get a truly understanding
response. When God had brought an end to my work at Teen Challenge and opened up the new work of Youth Outreach in California,
I took the first opportunity to have a long, heart-to-heart talk with
my old teacher, the Reverend Esteban Camarillo. I told him about
both of those times when the Evil One seemed so close. I left out
nothing, knowing that here was a man who would understand, perhaps even help me understand those shaking experiences.

When I had finished telling about them, I asked, "What do you
think, Reverend Camarillo? Is there any hope for me?"

"Nicky," said this man of God with a smile, "do you think you're
the only one the devil is after?"

"No, but these horrible thoughts were right *in my mind!* What kind of a person am I?"

"Nicky, you're the same kind of person as anyone else the devil has lost but is still trying to get back. First of all, think of where you were both those times. Right on the devil's turf, as you fellows would say! You were besting the devil at his own business, snatching human beings from his grip, and he doesn't like that! So like a roaring lion he comes after you.

"As to thoughts—Martin Luther used to say they're like birds. You can't help it if they fly over your head, but you don't need to let them build nests in your hair! Satan is a clever being, Nicky. I wish I could say there were never any evil thoughts in *my* mind, but I can't. One thing is for sure. When you called on God for help, you did exactly the right thing. Resist the devil and he has to flee from you. Resist him with God's help and you can't lose!

"Nicky, do you remember when Jesus was tempted? Look up the fourth chapter of Luke. Some say that Satan came to Him in bodily form; some say it was a mental or spiritual temptation. Whichever it was, even He was tempted by the devil, so is it surprising that you were?"

Since that talk with the Reverend Camarillo I have never been oppressed the same way again. And I have come to realize some other things about Satan. Jesus called him a liar and a murderer (John 8:44). Gloria is the one person on earth I love most, and is a tremendous help to me in every way. How Satan would like to destroy her—and me at the same time!

Another thing: Both times I was so oppressed by Satan, I had been fasting a lot. I was skin and bones, and now I realize I was overdoing the fasting. I still fast on special occasions, but I have come to realize an important secret of the Christian life. God wants us *strong* mentally, spiritually, and physically. When we become weak at any point, Satan tries to slip past our guard at that point. Important as fasting may sometimes be, the devil can use even that to try to get the better of us.

But I have come to an assurance about that. As I agonized about what had happened when I seemed to be almost back in the clutches of Satan, Jesus gave me a marvelous word of assurance. He said to me:

Nicky, there is no way the devil can have you. He will never stop trying, but so long as you trust Me, he will never be able to move you one fraction of an inch from the hollow of My hand.

When I read passages like John 10:27, 28, I realize that that promise is for everyone. And I'm glad that these things happened, horrible as they were to go through at the time. They have taught me how much you have to depend on Christ *all the time:*

Because you never know what Satan will try next!

7

"Satan Wants You"

Recently I got a letter in the handwriting of a teen-age girl. It said:

Dear Nicky,

If you ever had a satanic attack, did you feel horrible? I still feel like I'm going to go insane. I wish God would take me. I hate the way I'm living. My heart feels like it weighs a hundred tons. There is absolutely no youth meeting that I know of around here. I had a demon delivered from me. And ever since my attack, I feel like he is returned. I don't know why in the world God ever stuck us where we are now.

I feel like going somewhere in private and screaming at Satan. I *HATE* him. Seems like I can't feel God's presence even when I know He is here. I don't like what is happening. Oh, how I wish He would appear to me in human form. I've got to be delivered somehow.

Nicky, is there any way out? I need help something terrible.

BECKY

I understand how Becky feels. From the somewhat jumbled expressions in her letter I could piece together the experiences she had just been through. Evidently God had delivered her from demon possession, but without the strength and help of Christian fellowship, Becky felt Satan returning like a roaring lion for the prey he had lost—and she sent me that desperate SOS for help.

As I prayed for Becky I confessed that I too feel horrible when Satan attacks. And ever since I was led to write this book, I have felt his relentless attacks. My trip to Puerto Rico to gather material for the manuscript is a case in point.

When my plane took off for that visit with my mother, there was only one problem: I wasn't aboard!

I had made reservations three weeks before. Everything seemed set for the flight at one-thirty in the afternoon. I waited in Kennedy airport, and was just about to board, when a call came booming over the public address system: "Will Mr. Nicky Cruz please call Operator 14?"

Figuring it must be something important, I went to the nearest telephone and was soon talking to the director of one of the Nicky Cruz Youth Outreach Centers. A Christian businessman in the area had promised to underwrite the Center's mortgage—now ten days overdue. Could I get in touch with the businessman before the bank made things uncomfortable for the Center?

I had to call three different numbers before I reached the Christian businessman. He apologized for the tight cash flow that had slowed down his payments and promised to send what was needed immediately. Relieved that that was settled, I sprinted for the doorway that led to my plane—and found it closed. Through the big glass windows of the waiting room I could see the 747 wheeling down the runway toward takeoff.

The next plane I could get on brought me to San Juan late that night. Everything I had planned to do in Puerto Rico that afternoon had to be shelved.

Well, there was still something I could count on, I thought. I had reserved a car through an auto rental agency, to get from San Juan to Las Piedras to visit my mother. "We have a nice 1972 Mercury Cougar," the auto rental girl had told me, and I had said, "I'll take it."

But the girl at the rental desk in the San Juan airport looked baffled when I put down my bags and asked for my Cougar. "I don't understand it, Mr. Cruz," she said. "There's been some terrible mixup. That Cougar we were holding for you has been given to someone else."

"What else do you have?" I asked, wondering how such a thing could have happened.

"I'm terribly sorry," said the girl. "There's a very heavy demand for cars this week. I'm afraid there's nothing left."

"But I have a reservation!" I exclaimed in exasperation.

The girl apologized again, but the upshot of it was that I had to get a cab to my hotel. Then it was my turn to apologize to two editors who had come to Puerto Rico in connection with my book and had been waiting all afternoon to see me. They were very nice about it all, but I realized that valuable time for the making of this book was being lost forever.

That night, like the night before and the two nights that followed, I found sleep almost impossible. When I did doze off, I would wake up again face-to-face with a new black thought.

Nothing is working out right, something seemed to be saying. *Everything will go wrong — you'll see.*

"No!" I said aloud — only to be hit by another depressing thought: *You're getting into waters too deep for you. Your father knew better than to turn against us. Why don't you quit the way he did?*

I recognized this as much more falsehood than truth, but still it made an impact. Then another black thought swam out of the darkness, as though a spirit of hell were saying:

What difference do you think you can make anyway? More kids are getting lost every day than you could save in years. We're winning and you know it. Why don't you leave a lost cause while you can? I pulled a pillow around my ears, wishing I could shut out that demonic voice as easily as I could turn off the radio.

Then I had a horrible vision. I can still remember when David Wilkerson predicted in a radio broadcast that a great revival among young people would soon be underway. He saw it coming, and now we are in the midst of it. But now as I tossed on my hotel bed, I saw a vision of thousands of young people marching behind the banners of the occult: **astrology** . . . **Buddhism** . . . **spiritualism** . . . **Hare**

Krishna . . . fortune telling . . . Satan worship . . . reincarnation . . . Hinduism . . . yoga . . . meditation . . . magic . . . witchcraft! As David Wilkerson saw the first signs of the Jesus movement, I was seeing the advance signs of some of Satan's greatest delusions.

"Lord," I prayed, "help me to stay always behind Your banner. If You can use me, I'm ready."

Next morning I picked up the telephone and didn't put it down until the rental agency had promised to send over a car. It was slightly battered but decidedly better than nothing.

The two editors who had come to Puerto Rico had both brought their wives along. I invited all four to come along with me to Las Piedras. The car pulled annoyingly to the left as I drove, and I'm afraid I had some unkind thoughts about the rental agency.

On the outskirts of San Juan I turned into a winding driveway for the first stop. Luis Rosario, once a hopeless heroin addict, and his wife, Carmen, direct a Youth Outreach center whose purpose is to *prevent* kids from turning to drugs. I'm proud of what Luis and Carmen are doing. I wanted to pay them a short visit and show the visitors what Youth Outreach is doing in Puerto Rico.

As we came to the center at the end of the long driveway, however, everything was in an uproar. Carmen Rosario explained that three of the youngsters were out of their minds from a new way of getting high. They had taken the leaves of a *campana* plant, a Puerto Rican narcotic (sometimes called "Angel's Trumpet Tree"), boiled them, and drunk the "tea." As a result they were delirious.

I went to the room where the boys were being guarded—one of them kept calling "Mama!" and trying to throw himself out the window—and prayed for them. Carmen, always the perfect hostess, served the visitors refreshments and remarked, "None of the boys at the center has ever done anything like this before." But she was not quite as unruffled as she usually is, and I could imagine her wondering, "Why did you have to come at a time like this?" I myself was thinking, *A fine demonstration this is of keeping young people from drugs!* Of course, I knew it was no fault of the workers at the center.

Back on the road, I found the car still trying to pull to one side, but I was beginning to get used to that when the whole vehicle started bumping and vibrating and pulling off to the right. I put my foot on the brake and pulled off the road, discovering that the right front tire was as flat as a pancake. The tire had blown out so completely that the rubber remaining was mangled and tattered. I was mighty thankful we had been able to come to a safe stop.

The tropical sun beat down as everyone piled out of the car and the two men helped change the tire. We were just getting the spare tire into place when one of the men leaped into the air and started scratching and flailing his arms in all directions and shouting, "Something's biting me!" At the same time I felt dozens of tiny bites on my ankles — and around the waist — and on my arms! I looked down and could see tiny red ants crawling all over my wrists. As everyone began scratching and rubbing at the ants that were crawling over all of us, I looked down and saw thousands of the tiny red ants on the ground, especially right at my feet by the right front wheel. We were standing in the center of a mammoth anthill!

We brushed off ants as fast as we could and finished changing the tire in lightning speed. I wished I could pull off my clothes to get rid of the biting insects, and I know everyone else felt the same way. We had to be content with getting rid of as many ants as we could and getting out of there as fast as possible.

I had not wanted Mother to be worried about my trip to Las Piedras, so — as I often do — I simply dropped in without warning. I felt it was better this way, particularly since the subject was so important. But this time when I arrived with my four friends, it was my sister Carmen who answered my knock on the door.

"Nicky," Carmen said, "Mama is sick. She has not been well for two days."

Another blow! I had especially wanted the two editors and their wives to meet my mother, and it was vitally important to talk with her about the old days of witchcraft and spiritualism. I was making a quick silent prayer for Mama and wondering what to do when Mama walked out of her bedroom and hugged me.

All that afternoon Mother sat and answered my questions and those of my American friends. As she talked, her beautiful voice rising and falling in lilting Spanish, I kept marveling that she had arisen from a sickbed. But Mama is a very strong lady, and with God on her side there is little she cannot do.

We had a wonderful conversation with my mother on the porch of our Las Piedras house that afternoon. The four Americans asked questions which I put to Mother in Spanish and she answered in her vibrant, singing voice. We covered a lot of ground and filled in a lot of gaps in my memories. One of the editors had a tape recorder and got everything down on tape cassettes – I thought.

I would have been more worried if I had known that afternoon what I discovered later. The first cassette started unwinding and stopped recording halfway through the first side. When the editor discovered this, at least an hour's interviewing had been lost. Fortunately, he had also been scribbling penciled notes summarizing the conversation.

"I've never had anything like this happen before," the editor said when he told me about the lost recording.

That night, as I thought over my first day in Puerto Rico gathering material for this book, the day's events and those of the previous day unrolled in my memory like a television documentary:

- the overdue mortgage and the telephone call that resulted in my missing the plane.

- the car reservation that wasn't.

- the previous two sleepless nights and the depressing thoughts that had poured into my mind.

- the boys who had to get high on *campana* at the very time the five of us visited the Outreach center. (Such a thing had *never* happened before. Why *now?* Was the incident intended to discredit our work?)

- the bad car, the flat tire, and the ants. Why did that tire blow out so that we stopped at that particular spot – on top of a giant anthill?

- Mama's sickness.

- the fouled-up tape recorder.

Were all these things coincidences? What was going on?

I snapped on the light and opened my Bible to the first chapter of Job. I read again the ancient story of the calamities that had roared into the life of that good man. Almost all at the same time, desert raiders had stolen his livestock and killed his servants, lightning had struck and burned up his sheep, and a hurricane had flattened the house where every one of his children had been having dinner. If anything like that happened to anyone today, we would shake our heads and wonder how it could take place. But in the Book of Job, God takes us behind the scenes and shows us why such things happened. Satan was after Job, trying to claim him for his own, and he used the forces of nature and even human beings to try to make that good man fall!

But Satan hadn't been able to do a single thing against Job and his family except with the permission of God. The devil has horrifying power, and yet there is always a point at which God says, "This far you can come—but no farther!" The devil could use a mighty wind, fire from heaven, and lawless racketeers for his awful purposes. Later, as the Book of Job shows in the following chapters, the devil touched Job himself first with a horrible disease and then with a blasphemous suggestion from his wife. She was always trying to get Job to curse his Creator. But beaten and bruised as Job was, he never gave in—and God still guarded him!

I thought of the Scripture passage Gloria and I had read recently in our family devotions. At the Last Supper, just before Peter denied him, Jesus had warned, "Simon, Simon, behold, Satan hath desired to have you . . ." (Luke 22:31). Or: "Peter, Satan wants you!" *Of course* Satan would want that natural leader of the twelve apostles to fall. What a prize that would have been for hell! But that wasn't all Jesus had said to Peter! He had added: "But I have prayed for thee, that thy faith fail not . . ." (v. 32). What a wonderful Saviour we have. He is praying for all of us, and He is not going to let the tempter have us, if we keep trusting and obeying!

I remembered the telephone conversation one of the editors had told me he'd had recently with John Sherrill. When John, who co-authored *The Cross and the Switchblade* and *The Hiding Place* and other wonderful books, learned of the publication plans for *Satan on the Loose,* he phoned the editor with a word of counsel.

"Be prepared for all kinds of opposition," John Sherrill warned. "Satan usually strikes us at our weakest points. And you never know what he may try. Recently, while I was working on an article about demon possession, every appliance in our house broke down!"

Then John Sherrill prayed over the telephone for God's blessing on the writing and publication of this book. "Lord," he prayed, "help us to remember that although Satan goes about like a roaring lion, he has false teeth, for when we resist him, he has to flee!"

That was a wonderful thought as I reflected on the age-old warfare between the devil and the Lord. I have no doubt whatever that Satan is "the god of this world," as the Bible says. But that night as I thought about his attempts to interfere with the writing of this book, I was immensely thankful for the Omnipotent God who had foiled every one of his recent attacks. Though I had missed the plane I had planned to take to San Juan, I had arrived safely on the later one. Although there was no Cougar awaiting me at the airport, I did get a car to Las Piedras. While that one was in poor shape, all of us got where we needed to in spite of the flat tire and the ants!

The *campana* disaster simply showed the kinds of problems our outreach centers have to be equipped to deal with these days, and the effectiveness of our Puerto Rican staff. Mama had been ill, but the Lord had brought her a marvelous healing at just the right time. If the tape recorder had failed to function temporarily, the material from my mother lived on in the written notes and the memories of those present.

And God could handle sleep-threatening nights, too. With that realization I rolled over as though onto a mattress of clouds, and went into a deep sleep secure in my Father's powerful, supporting love.

During that second night in Puerto Rico a friend of mine had a strange experience. When he told me about it, I realized it had come to him the same night I was so oppressed by all the things I've just mentioned. Here is his experience:

About two o'clock at night, my friend told me, he woke up with a feeling he had never had before. He felt an evil presence drawing near, pleading:

Don't you feel sorry for me? I am condemned to eternal punishment for something that happened long ago. Pity me! If there were some end to this punishment, but there is none. Don't you see how much I need your sympathy? Help me!

"This was definitely not a dream," my friend said. "I was wide awake. In fact, I checked the clock to see what time it was. At first I did feel sorry for the condemned spirit that seemed to be speaking to me. Then I realized that any sympathy for a demon was distrust of the wisdom and justice of my heavenly Father. And if I can't trust Him, who can I trust?

"Nicky, I've never thought much about evil spirits before, but this experience was as clear and definite as anything that ever happened to me. There are few people I would tell this to; if someone told the same thing to me, I might question his sanity, we're all so far away from what the New Testament tells us about the spirit world. But I think you will understand it, Nicky. Put this in your book if you want to. Maybe it will help convince someone else that the invisible world the Bible describes is as real as anything visible — actually more real."

While I was at the San Juan airport waiting for my plane back to New York, a young woman who looked about thirty years old came stalking over to where I was sitting and gritted at me through clenched teeth: "I hate your guts!"

Stunned, I tried to figure out what had brought that on. While I was wondering, she burst into a torrent of vile language.

"You claim you're a Christian. Curse everyone that follows that weak sniveling imitation of a religion. You're a phony, Nicky Cruz, just like everyone that tries to ram Christianity down somebody else's throat! Your God isn't worth anything. The real god is the devil. He's the one I pray to, the one with the real power and the action. I'm going to put a curse on you that you'll never get rid of!"

And with that this young lady, who looked like a hundred other young women except for the hate in her face and the unclean fury in her blazing eyes, stared at me with a cold malevolent hatred such as I haven't seen since I was in a rumble in the slums of New York.

I understood what she was trying to do. She was trying to psych me out—to frighten me out of my trust in God with a psychological attack. I could feel waves of hostility pouring toward me, but I wasn't worried.

And I wasn't going to fall into her trap and return hate for hate, either. I remembered the amazing love that had broken down my own hatred years ago, and I smiled at this young woman and said: "You know that what you're saying isn't true at all. But I don't think I know you. Who are you?"

Silence, as those eyes, filled with hate, bored into mine.

"Lady," I said, "I'm going to pray for you. I'm going to pray to the God who is all love and all-powerful, the God who loves me so much that He covers me with the protective blood of Jesus, that He will show you the only safe place is under the blood. In the name of Jesus I call on you to turn to Him now!"

The woman's face contorted with fury. "Hogwash!" she screamed. Then she whirled around and disappeared into the crowd of travelers.

When I left Puerto Rico I had to fly from New York to Detroit for a youth rally there. It so happened that my good friends Lou and Lana Rawls were in that city at the time, and I had dinner with them before I left.

Afterward, as my cab was speeding along the expressway to the Detroit airport, it suddenly began to slow down. I heard screeching brakes behind me as the speedometer needle slowed to 40 . . . 35 . . . 30 . . . 25. "Pull over to the right!" I shouted to the driver. As he did so a gigantic truck swerved past us; it must have been going at least 70 miles an hour. I noticed beads of perspiration on the driver's forehead.

"I don't know what's happening!" he said. "Nothing like this ever happened before!"

I could see that his right foot was clear to the floorboards.

Then, without any apparent reason, the needle on the speedometer slowly climbed back up to 55 and we got to the airport. When I got out the driver was still mumbling and shaking his head. He didn't have any idea what had been going on.

I can't say *I* didn't have!

But as I flew out of Detroit I kept thinking of the incredible story Lou and Lana had just told me about events in their home in Encino, California. It was amazing how it all fitted into what I had just been through.

8

The Invaders

Satan has been working vigorously in America to imbed his principles and himself in people and places all over the country. He has reached into thousands and thousands of hearts and homes. Even though I have seen this movement so clearly in the last few years, I was still surprised when I heard from two of my own personal friends how the Liar had invaded their lives.

I was enjoying a fantastic steak dinner with Lou and Lana Rawls in Detroit one evening right after my trip to Puerto Rico. The discussions with my mother about witchcraft and my own experiences with the demonic were still on my mind, so I brought the subject up as we ate. When I mentioned the word "spirits," Lou and Lana quickly glanced at each other as if I'd struck upon a touchy subject. I realized soon that I had definitely done just that!

Neither Lou nor Lana had had easy lives — before or after their marriage. Lana went to a Catholic boarding school when she was ten and had been left with the full responsibility of her younger brother, Larry, while she was still a teen-ager. To provide for him and herself, she worked as a "bunny" at the age of seventeen. She had to grow up fast; but she never deserted the high moral standards of her early training.

At eighteen she met Lou. He was several years older than Lana and just beginning his singing career. The two fell deeply in love—love that has brought them through many difficult times together. Although interracial marriages are still not very popular, they are accepted more readily than they were thirteen years ago when Lana and Lou were wed. To be black is beautiful now. Lou and Lana have been condemned, cursed, rejected, and literally persecuted by blacks and whites alike. But through all of the anguish and loneliness, Lana has stayed beside Lou, encouraging him and loving him. That bond of love that began when they were so young has been strengthened by time and testing. Lana and Lou have come through the thick and thin of the entertainment world, often having only each other to cling to for support. It's not surprising that "Love Is A Hurting Thing" is one of Lou's favorite songs.

Their struggle together is probably one reason that Lana and Lou are still down-to-earth people, even though Lou is a well-known name in the entertainment industry. Lou grew up in the ghetto, and he remembers well the hard life. He has a special place in his heart for underprivileged kids and has shown it time after time in high-school benefits. He knows "where they're at," and reaches into their lives to share himself with them. Lou expresses himself so vividly in his music. He "feels" his songs, in a way similar to the way I "feel" my sermons. He pours his heart and soul into every song he sings, and this quality had made him into the outstanding performer he is. It also keeps him the warm, feeling person he is.

Lana shares the same naturalness and warmth once she knows you. Because she has been misjudged and mistreated so often, she is cautious about revealing the real Lana to a new acquaintance. Her marriage to Lou, her eye-catching clothes, even her false eyelashes have caused many religious people to shun her—or invite her to the altar for prayer! But those who so quickly judge know nothing about the heart. The same is true of Lou. He is often criticized because of his activities in the entertainment world. But I know both of them well—the "real Rawls"—and they are beautiful people for whom I praise the Lord!

So that night in Detroit, when the two of them began to tell of their ordeal, I was thoroughly surprised to hear how my friends had gone through just the kind of experiences that had been on my mind. After they had exchanged that knowing look at each other, Lou said, "Let's tell him."

Lana explained: "Nicky, we've been through some things we've hardly dared tell anyone about. Most people would think we were off our rockers!"

"At first," Lou said with a grin, "when Lana began telling me about Mr. Benson I wondered if she ought to see a psychiatrist!" He shook his head. "Even after seeing it with my own eyes, it's still hard to believe."

The whole thing began, they told me, when they moved into their present home in Encino. Their house is one of those architectural works of art you often see in California, especially in or near Hollywood—a 90 percent glass, twenty-two-room mansion set on an estate of lush gardens, tropical trees, and flowers of every kind and color. The house is situated on top of a hill overlooking the city of Los Angeles. At night, looking out across the city, the thousands of lights from the city twinkling and dancing below remind you of a Christmas tree. It seems the whole world is at your feet; you are in a castle, gazing down on your kingdom.

Lou had just left the house one morning when Lana's brother, Larry, who was staying with them, came into the kitchen looking white around the mouth. After he had gulped down a cup of coffee, he burst out, "This is the funniest place I've ever been in."

"What do you mean, Larry?" asked Lana.

"When I woke up this morning I felt like I was suffocating. There was a pillow over my head and it seemed like someone was pushing it down onto my face. I couldn't breathe! At first I thought it was some practical joker."

When Larry paused, Lana asked, "Well, what was it? Don't keep me in suspense!"

"That's just it," said Larry with a worried frown. "I managed to push the pillow away—and no one was there."

Lana said, "You've got to be kidding."

But he wasn't—and that was only the first of a whole series of incredible events at the Rawls's house!

Soon afterward Lou's niece, Tiny, who was also staying there at the time, told Lana she had often felt that someone was in her room at night. "Several times my door opened and closed just like someone was coming into the room," Tiny said, "but no one was there. I was scared to tell anyone because I thought you'd all laugh at me."

As Lana and Lou went on with their story, the waiter (who had come with a fresh pot of coffee) stood with the pot in his hands — staring. At first I thought he was simply looking at Lana. She is the type of woman who gets the attention of *everyone* in a room the moment she enters. She is very shapely and has a very feminine look — the kind of blue-eyed blond that anyone might find it hard not to ogle. But then I realized that the man was apparently hypnotized by the story, not Lana. Finally he came to himself, set down the coffeepot, and left, but I didn't wonder that he was fascinated.

Lana, explaining more about the house itself, said that when it is very foggy or stormy outside, you get a very eerie, strange feeling. When Lana was recovering from a serious operation, she was bedridden for six weeks. At that time a wonderful Christian woman, George Ann Tenney, came and cared for Lana's two children, Louanna and Lou, Jr. George Ann has a keen sense of discernment, and the very first time she entered that house, she got a strange feeling, as if the house were evil. She went from room to room, pleading the blood of Jesus for protection.

One night, Lou said, the front door opened and closed while the family was in the living room, just as though an invisible man had come in. Another night the two were getting ready for bed when Lana rolled down the covers of their circular bed, which is usually topped with TV pillows. Lana put the TV pillow on her side of the bed on the floor while Lou was brushing his teeth in the bathroom. When Lou, Jr., who hates bedtime, called Lana, she went to his room to tuck him in. Returning, she found her TV pillow back on the bed.

"Lou!" Lana called as her husband came back from the bathroom. "What's going on here?"

When Lana pointed out that her pillow had mysteriously popped back on the bed, Lou was baffled.

That night Lana lay awake for a long time while everyone else in the house slept. As she mulled over the strange recent events, the thought came to her mind: *There is a spirit in this house and he is exposing himself.*

"Why, that's ridiculous," thought Lana. But the idea would not go away.

In the middle of the night, when everyone else was asleep, Lana heard the clatter of pots and pans. In the morning the kitchen was a bizarre sight. A heavy frying pan was in the middle of the floor. A large pressure cooker lay on its side behind the refrigerator, the coffeepot was in the sink, and knives and forks were scattered in odd corners of the kitchen.

"What was going on here last night?" Bea Bea, the housekeeper, asked Lana.

"That's what I'd like to know," retorted Lana as she helped Bea Bea put the things where they belonged. When Lou came in he refused to believe the girls' story. "All this is getting to be just too much," he said.

That was exactly the way Lana felt a little later when Lou went to Chicago for a series of singing engagements. She planned to meet him there, and take him a leather jacket she had bought for him in Spain. The morning she was to leave, Lana got the jacket out of the clothes closet and hung it on the back of a fish-shaped chair in a corner of the bedroom. After breakfast, as she finished packing, Lana turned to pick up the jacket to pack into her suitcase. As she reached to the back of the chair, the jacket was gone.

She called Bea Bea and asked, "Did you take Lou's jacket?" Bea Bea was as mystified as Lana over the strange disappearance. The leather jacket was nowhere to be found. Finally Lana left without it, locking the bedroom door as she went out.

When Lou and Lana returned home and unlocked the bedroom door, Lou asked, "What did you mean, my jacket disappeared? It was right there all the time!"

There, on the back of the fish-shaped chair, where Lana had put it originally, was the leather jacket. Only it hadn't been there *all* the time, as Lana and Bea Bea well knew.

The Rawls's home had once been owned by a well-to-do gentleman named Benson. Neighbors told Lana and Lou that Mr. Benson used to love to lie in the round sunken tub in the bathroom and enjoy the sunshine that pours through the wide glass doors. Mr. Benson, now dead, had a wife who was slim, blond, and blue-eyed—not unlike Lana.

Desiring more privacy, Lana called in an interior decorator, John Warden, to put a curtain in front of the glass doors. He put up a massive curtain rod and came back the next day to hang the curtain. That morning, while Lana was tending the clothing shop which she and Lou own and manage, she got an excited telephone call from John Warden.

"Mrs. Rawls," asked Warden, "did someone break into your house last night?"

"Break into the house? Not as far as I know. Why?"

"That big curtain rod," said John Warden, "has been bent clear out of shape."

"You can't be serious!" exclaimed Lana.

He was. The rod, Lou and Lana discovered when they inspected it that night, had been bent into a circle. Lana said, "It's been bent back to where they say Mr. Benson's drapes used to be."

She and Lou remembered several other changes they had made in the house—all of which had been mysteriously resisted.

Lana declared: "This has got to stop." She raised her voice. "Mr. Benson, that new curtain rod is going to stay where we put it. I want you to quit this nonsense."

Lana and Lou have been trying to sell their house for the past two years, but with no success. Everytime the realtors put the FOR SALE sign up on the front lawn, it was found the next morning in the bed of ivy. This has occurred about twenty times—Lana calls the real estate agency to put up a new sign, and the next morning it is found on the ground. Finally the agency put up a very strong, sturdy metal sign and dug the legs deep down into the ground and bolted it down from the top. Not even a strong wind could have moved it; however, the next morning it was found once more in the bed of ivy.

"Nicky," said Lana, "I can send you a picture of the sign tomorrow. As God is my witness, that sign is down there right now in the ivy."

As Lana and Lou continued telling me more of the incredible events that had taken place in their home, I was dumbfounded. I know Lou and Lana. I knew they would never merely make this story up. I could tell by the expression on their faces and in their voices that what they had experienced was real — very real.

In 1969, Lana, like many other Californians, had been worried over the widespread predictions that an earthquake was about to shake the State of California into the ocean. She confided these fears to an astrologer friend who told her: "Lana, you are the type of person who attracts spirits. Don't ever light candles — they draw spirits to someone like you."

Lana and Lou's bedroom is very large, with an extremely high ceiling, large windows, and a door opening onto a patio. The room has very plush decor done in various shades of pink chiffon and velvet. A magnificent chandelier hangs directly over a round bed, pink chiffon curtains are hanging that can be drawn around the bed — giving the appearance of a "harem bed."

One night Lana and Lou were in their bedroom. Lou had put on some soft romantic music and Lana had turned out all the lights and lit some beautiful candles they had received as a gift. The entire room was aglow with the hazy candlelight. The two were having an intimate conversation and were lying in the bed with the chiffon curtains drawn so they completely surrounded the bed. The entire setting gave the impression of a coffin — as if Lana were in a casket. I am sure she wasn't thinking of it at the time but she says, "As I look back now, I am sure that would have been the impression a person would have gotten upon entering the room."

Lou turned to Lana and saw that suddenly her face had become panic-stricken. She had a desperate look in her eyes. She began gasping for air and trying to scream but could only whisper, "I feel like I'm having a heart attack. Help me! Help me!"

She felt as if she was being smothered. She tried to keep calm, but it was too much.

"What's happening?" Lou frantically exclaimed. He became panicky. "What do you want me to do — call an ambulance? Let me help you!"

But Lana, desperately trying to yell, said in a hoarse voice, "Don't touch me! Blow out the candles! Blow out the candles!"

She kept repeating, "Blow out the candles!" as she crawled to the end of the bed and yanked open the curtains. Then she slipped off the bed and literally crawled on her hands and knees across the bedroom floor out to the patio. As Lou extinguished all the candles, Lana's breathing started to return to normal.

Recovering somewhat, Lana got up and slowly walked over to the edge of the patio overlooking the city below. Still in a daze, she peered out into the darkness and the city lights. As she stood there, shaken from the traumatic experience, she remembered how she had felt—that her life was being drawn away and she was being taken to a horrible place from which she would never return. Then the warning from the astrologer about the candles returned to her mind. She had felt perfectly fine before the "attack" and hadn't had any recent illnesses, and yet suddenly, with no warning, she couldn't breathe. As the cool night breezes blew against her body and hair, questions began to flow through her mind. *"Why?* Why, Lou?" Lana asked over and over.

One evening Lana came home and found Larry, Fern (a good friend of the family), and several of Larry's friends in the living room playing with a Ouija board. She didn't know much about this so-called game and although she is a Christian, she wasn't aware of its evil power.

"Lana," urged Larry, "come and sit down with us and ask some questions. Talk to Mr. Benson on the Ouija board."

Lana thought of the bizarre experiences she had had in the past. "But the Ouija is just a game," she said.

"No, it isn't," said Larry. "It's surprising what you can find out sometimes from a Ouija board."

(Let me repeat: Ouija is a *very* dangerous game. No one should have anything to do with it, as Lana and Larry now know.)

Lana sat down with the rest of the group around the Ouija board and started questioning it. As you may know, Ouija operates when those present rest their fingertips very lightly on a plastic disk which answers questions by moving to various points on the board. A typical Ouija board contains all the letters of the alphabet, the nine numerals, and the words YES, NO, and GOODBYE.

The session began with simple questions: "Is it daytime?" The disk correctly shot to the word NO.

"What time is it?"

Quickly the disk moved to the numerals 9:55 and the letters P.M.

"Do you know my children?" asked Lana.

The disk spelled out their initials.

"Who do I work for?"

(The Ouija board refused to spell my name—I employ Lana as a public-relations director. Perhaps this is because I am a Christian and a preacher—or maybe it was jealous of me.)

"Is my employer married?"

YES

"What is his wife's name?"

G–L–O–R–I–A C–R–U–Z

"Do they have any children?"

YES–3 GIRLS

"Are you Mr. Benson?"

YES

"Are you here?"

YES

"If you are actually present," Lana said, "I want you to reveal yourself right now."

Then something happened that is difficult to explain. Lana has many green plants in her living room and when she asked the spirit to reveal itself, immediately the fronds of the palm trees gently stirred. Although all the windows were closed, the trees slightly swayed to and fro. Lana didn't really become scared because she felt the assurance that Jesus Christ was with her.

Lana continued questioning: "Are you jealous?"

YES

"Who are you jealous of?"

The disk spelled: LOU

(Perhaps I should add here that Lana, as suggested previously, is very beautiful, with creamy white skin, blue eyes, and blond hair. Lou stands nearly six feet tall, every inch a gentleman, attractive, and with tremendous charisma. And Lou has made it to the top as a recording artist.)

As Lana watched the board spell LOU, she remembered the number of times Lou had said he had telephoned her and no one had answered. After several of these incidents, someone discovered the telephone volume had been moved to the lowest point. She asked the Ouija board, "Did you turn the phone down?"

YES

"Are you in love with me?"

YES

"Have you ever made love to me?"

YES

"How many times?"

The Ouija board disk moved rapidly over all the numerals as though it lost count.

"Are you jealous of men in my house?"

YES

"Have you made love to other women in my house?"

YES

"Who have you never made love to?"

FERN

Fern is an attractive young girl who has sometimes stayed overnight at the Rawls's. Perhaps the reason her name was spelled out is that she is a virgin.

"Would you ever try to hurt me?"

NO

"Would you ever use Lou to hurt me?"

YES

Then Lana began to recall how her white poodle, Fufu, followed her everywhere she went. If she walked fifteen miles a day, Fufu would be right beside her. When Lana would bathe, Fufu would sit on the second step of her sunken bathtub watching her. Every night, Fufu would sleep with Lana. And whenever she went out of town, the poodle would hide and cry for hours.

"Have you ever possessed my dog, Fufu?" Lana asked the Ouija.

YES

The Ouija board was apparently giving accurate answers to every question it was asked. Lana began to be frightened because she realized this "game" was no joke. More afraid than ever of whatever it was that apparently had a jealous spirit and destructive, murderous intentions, Lana fell to her knees and began praying: "O God, I don't want to be possessed by any spirit but Your Spirit. Please help me. Amen."

Immediately the disk shot to the word GOODBYE and then shot right off the board, bouncing onto the floor.

Lana said good-night and went to her bedroom and prayed, falling into a peaceful sleep.

Meanwhile, as the others continued playing Ouija, they heard someone breathing over the intercom system. (The Rawls's house has an intercom in every room but it is *always* turned off at night.) At first the players thought that Lana was playing a joke on them. However, when Larry opened the door to Lana's room, she was sound asleep; yet the breathing noise continued. Larry ran from room to room, checking the intercom system, and found that each unit was off. One of Larry's friends, who still could not believe what he saw and heard happening, told the spirit that if it were actually real to reveal itself at 2:00 A.M. At exactly 2:00 A.M., the plants in the living room began moving. As the plants began swaying and moving, the piano in one corner of the room began playing — not a song, but just a tinkling, the keys lightly moving. Although there were no windows open, the group could feel a wind in the room. Larry ran to his bedroom and got his Bible and began reading it. The mysterious movement of plants and the tinkling of the piano stopped as he pled the blood of Jesus.

Lana was raised a strict Catholic, yet she never had a personal encounter with Jesus until about two and a half years ago. At one of my crusades she gave her heart to Jesus. Since that time she has been a changed person. She reads her Bible, and prayer is very real to her. She seeks God's guidance in her life.

Lou was raised in the Chicago ghetto, yet he has a good knowledge of the faith because as a boy, his grandmother, who was a very dedicated Christian, would read him parts of the Bible. Lou definitely loves the Lord, hard as it is for anyone in the public eye as he is to stand always for Him. Since the first time I heard about "Mr. Benson" I have spent much time in discussion and prayer with Lou and Lana.

"You know," I said one night when I was at their house, "it just isn't possible for a person's spirit to float around on earth after death. Jesus promised the thief who repented on the cross next to His, 'This day shalt thou be with me in paradise.' After the rich man in Jesus' parable died, he begged permission to go back to earth to warn his brothers not to follow him to hell, but it was not permitted for him to cross the gulf.

"I don't doubt you've been troubled by a spirit, but I cannot believe it is Mr. Benson's. The devil is a liar and deceiver, you know. It looks to me as if you've been disturbed by a spirit entity that's been trying to confuse you. All the evidence shows that evil spirits have many of the characteristics of psychotics. They are deceptive, unpredictable, sometimes irrationally destructive. Some of the things that happened here Satan may have engineered simply to draw you away from Christ. How he would love to have you believe in a spirit world in place of heaven and hell! How he would love to have you believe in him instead of Christ!"

Lou and Lana asked me to pray that the spirit would depart. So we all joined together as I prayed:

"Lord, fill this house from top to bottom with Your love and grace. May Lou and Lana and all that dwell here look only to You for help and guidance. Fill them all with Your Spirit, and deliver them from every kind of evil. Let the blood of Jesus keep them safe forever. Amen."

"You know, Nicky," said Lana, "ever since you prayed for us that night, we haven't heard from 'Mr. Benson.' Our house is covered by the blood of Jesus Christ and nothing can harm us."

Lou has done several vocal numbers for Oral Roberts's television program and Oral and Lou have become good friends. When Oral was in town doing a recording for one of his programs, Lou invited him home. While he was in their home, the couple told the evangelist of their experiences with spirits. Oral, too, prayed that Lana and Lou would have complete deliverance from evil spirits. He reminded them that Jesus came to give us total victory over the devil. All we have to do is claim it and there is truly power through His precious blood.

Lou and Lana's experience makes me think of the television series "The Invaders." The invaders are alien beings from another planet who come to the earth and try to conquer it. In the process they try to either dominate or destroy anyone who realizes what they are doing.

The fact is that there *are* invaders, more terrifying than any television writer can imagine, dedicated to gaining control of the earth! They want to delude or dominate all of us. If they can't do it, they try to destroy.

9

The Demon Dimension

How do you explain things like that? My father's psychic powers, my mother's occult gifts, my own contacts with the demonic world, the experiences of Lou and Lana—how can they be explained?

There are plenty of theories about the occult. But the only explanation that really makes sense to anyone like myself who has so much firsthand knowledge, is the one I found when I first got a Bible from David Wilkerson and started reading it. I began at the first verse of Genesis and everything I read was like turning on a light in a dark room. I was amazed to find how much it explained: the beginning of the world, the beginning of life, the beginning of human beings and the beginning of *evil*.

When you mention the devil many people think of a repulsive being, but they're only half right. What struck me hardest when I started reading Genesis was how attractive the serpent was. Adam and Eve would never have fallen for Satan's lies if they could have seen him in his hideous nakedness. He knew better than to show them what he was really like. So he entered into the body of a glittering serpent, which at that time could move upright and was not the crawling creature it later became, and he spoke to Eve with all the appeals of Madison Avenue.

There is a woman in the United States today who has been obsessed for years with someone or something that came to her, she says, while she was experimenting with a Ouija board. When this entity first made itself known to her she said she had never been so caught "between curiosity and caution, so fascinated and baffled." Today this woman is making a career out of the spirit that comes over her, speaks in a deep male voice, and lectures about all kinds of occult subjects. The way it got hold of her is the way Satan got hold of Eve. Check the third chapter of Genesis and see for yourself. You'll find he is still using the same tricks to try to get hold of all of us! He knows how to fascinate, attract, possess.

When I first read Genesis 3, everything it said about Satan sprang out at me from the pages of the Bible. The devil was a strong influence—someone to keep away from! He took the form of a creature that anyone could see and touch. And he contradicted what God had said. My own experiences with Satan had been so real, I saw the danger in listening to him. His temptation of Adam and Eve reminded me vividly of my own confrontations with him. At the same time, as a new Christian I realized I would have to steer clear of his influence and even anything that had the appearance of any connection with him.

People defending witchcraft will tell you it's "the old religion." They argue that it was here before Christianity as though that made it better. But there is some truth in what they say, as there is a little truth in every good lie—that's what makes people believe it. Evil spirits have been around for a long time, as the very first pages of the Bible show.

Nowadays some of the airlines are advertising occult tours of England and India. As I was working on this book I took an occult tour of the Bible. What I did was to go right through it and stop at every place where it mentions the demonic world. Let me take you along as I share this occult tour with you.

There's a puzzling passage in the sixth chapter of Genesis that sets the stage for the Flood. It's puzzling because it's so much like today. Here is how The Living Bible paraphrases it:

Now a population explosion took place upon the earth. It was at this time that beings from the spirit world looked upon the beautiful earth women and took any they desired to be their wives. Then Jehovah said, "My Spirit must not forever be disgraced in man, wholly evil as he is. I will give him 120 years to mend his ways."

In those days, and even afterwards, when the evil beings from the spirit world were sexually involved with human women, their children became giants, of whom so many legends are told. When the Lord God saw the extent of human wickedness, and that the trend and direction of men's lives were only towards evil, he was sorry he had made them. It broke his heart. Genesis 6:1–6

Look at it: Human beings multiplying as never before; an occult explosion to match the population explosion; evil exploding everywhere; and some kind of unimaginable sexual involvement between evil spirits and evil humans. Don't ask me to explain all that. It happened before the first great judgment of the earth through the ancient Flood.

With so many events like that happening today, is it hard to believe that once more the stage is being set for the final judgment of Planet Earth?

Come over now to the Book of Exodus. There you read about how the Egyptians tried to wipe out the people of God, the Jewish race. What was behind that? Jesus said the devil is a liar and "a murderer from the beginning" (John 8:44). Satan's whole purpose is to deceive and destroy, *destroy*, DESTROY. He used violence against the Jews, as he instigated violence before the flood and as violence seems to be increasing so fast today. (Just look at how fast crime and acts of violence are growing right now everywhere.)

As you know, God saved the baby Moses from the Egyptians' mass murder of the Jewish babies. He hid him away until His moment came for redemption. Then he brought Moses out of the wilderness to make Pharaoh let the people go free. And as you probably also remember, God gave Moses certain signs to convince Pharaoh that He meant business. When Pharaoh demanded a miracle, Moses' brother Aaron threw his staff to the ground and it turned into a serpent.

Now Pharaoh had magicians or sorcerers who were pretty good.

They did the same thing with their own staffs. Then Aaron's staff swallowed theirs!

When Satan unleashes his power, God releases His power—and God's is always the greatest! Things are happening today that I can't explain, any more than I can explain all the things my father and mother did under spirit influence, but I have tested God's power and Satan's power and I have no question in my mind that God's power is the greatest of all.

Once God had forced the Egyptians to set the Israelites free and they were crossing the deserts to the Promised Land, they started grumbling and complaining against Moses and God. They didn't like their food, they longed for the leeks and garlic they were used to in Egypt, they doubted that they would make it through the wilderness. Complaints, complaints, complaints! Where did their spirit of criticism and doubt come from?

The thirty-second chapter of Exodus tells of one of the strangest chapters in the story. When Moses didn't come down from Mount Sinai right away, after he had gone to commune there with God, the Israelites asked Aaron to make them a new god to lead them! Incredibly, Aaron—the brother of Moses who had stood by his side all the way up to this point—agreed, and collected gold jewelry to make an idol of the new god. Then all the people worshiped it and celebrated with wild orgies.

Soon afterward Aaron and Miriam—the sister who had saved Moses' life when he was just a baby—criticized Moses so scathingly that God Himself condemned them (Numbers 12:1–14).

How did all this come about? The New Testament teaches us that the gods and idols of the heathen are devils or demons (1 Corinthians 10:20). When the Israelites worshiped an idol, they were putting themselves into subjection to the devil. And the very word *devil* means "accuser" or "slanderer," "one who speaks against." He accuses the Christian brothers night and day (Revelation 12:10). But how could the spirit of Satan get into the Israelites, especially into Aaron and Miriam, those stout co-workers with Moses?

When Agnes Sanford, a missionary's daughter, was a little girl in China, she went into a Buddhist temple and folded her hands and made the prayer before the statue of Buddha that she had heard the monks muttering. Nothing seemed to happen, she says in her book *Sealed Orders* — but from that time on she became aware of something strange within her, a sneering, scornful, inner voice.

Many years later Agnes Sanford met a minister who prayed for her and laid his hands on her head. With that the mental depression that had been troubling her went away, and she sang and shouted all the way home. She believes that when she made that childish prayer to Buddha she may well have opened her mind to demonic power, the same as someone may lay himself open to demon possession by experimenting with occult things like Ouija or astrology. And it takes all the power of God to drive such demons out.

The Bible and Christian experience testify that God is not far from any of us — and neither is Satan! The devil is always after anyone he thinks he can get hold of.

Are there prophets today making all kinds of predictions, some of them predictions of things that come true? There were in Bible times. Some of the prophets then, as now, tried to influence people to follow false religions. God warned in Deuteronomy: "If there is a prophet among you, or one who claims to foretell the future by dreams, and if his predictions come true but he says, 'Come, let us worship the gods of the other nations,' don't listen to him . . ." (13:1–3 LB).

Also, God warns that if a prophet says something will happen and it doesn't, the prophet's message is false and what he says is not from God (Deuteronomy 18:21, 22). If we followed what God says here, a lot of Americans would pay a lot less attention to the self-styled prophets and prophetesses who are always predicting the future.

One of the most fascinating characters in the Bible is King Saul. There were times when the Spirit of God came upon this gifted leader (1 Samuel 11:6). But there were other times when an evil spirit filled him, and he became rebellious, jealous, and murderous! (1 Samuel 15:20–23; 16:14; 18:9, 10; 19:9).

So it was with Gideon. While the Holy Spirit possessed him at one time and he became one of the greatest judges in Israel, at another time an evil spirit seized him and led him into sin (Judges 6:31ff.; 8:27).

Toward the end of his life, Saul became frantic when he was afraid the multitudes of Philistines would conquer the Israelites. Like many people who get immersed in the occult, Saul decided he just had to know what was going to happen. And knowing that God had threatened death to anyone involved in fortune telling, Saul disguised his appearance and went to a medium or witch at night. When he asked her to bring up the spirit of the dead prophet Samuel, the medium screamed, realizing the visitor was the king. (She was afraid he would have her killed for practicing witchcraft.)

The way the Bible describes this is very interesting (1 Samuel 28). In the words of the Living Bible, "When the woman saw Samuel, she screamed, 'You've deceived me! You are Saul!' " (v. 12). It sounds as though the woman were an imposter. She made her living tricking people into thinking they were communicating with the dead—as many people make money today. But then *she saw Samuel*. She must not have expected the prophet to show up, for when she saw him she screamed to Saul, "You've deceived me!"

Bible scholars don't agree about what actually happened there. One possibility is that an evil spirit appeared, impersonating Samuel. Another possibility is that God stepped in and let His messenger Samuel return from the beyond to tell Saul the truth about the future. Saul must have wished he had never asked what was going to happen, for Samuel told him very accurately that the next day his side would lose the battle and that he and all his sons would be dead. If Samuel himself appeared, it was one of the few times in history that anyone returned from death, for God is not going to let His saints be called out of heaven by mediums and necromancers who disobey His commands to have nothing to do with the occult.

Saul's experience always reminds me of my father and those who came to him for help. But my father had never known God when he was dealing with spirits. Saul knew God, knew the ways of the Lord, knew His love and grace, and yet sought light from a woman who professed to communicate with the dead. When I first read of the witch of Endor it amazed me—it still does—that a man who knew such a better way would turn to a person who was working for the devil! How could Saul depend on a witch when he knew the ways of the Lord?

This Bible passage and the one about the serpent tempting Adam and Eve are just as vivid to me today as when I first read them. Their truths are still deeply embedded in my heart—the power of Satan, the wickedness of Satan, and man's foolishness in putting any confidence whatsoever in Satan!

Saul insisted on knowing what God withholds—knowledge of the future. If any of us knew all that would happen to us, we would be obsessed by the problems and troubles of the future, and finally by our own death. We don't need to know those things. God withholds such knowledge in His mercy. Our future is in His loving hands, and we ought to be content to leave it there. If we make the most of each moment as it comes, and live and trust in Him, it doesn't matter what happens tomorrow, because nothing can ever separate us from His love and care.

When David became king of Israel, a glorious era began—but notice how fast David went downhill spiritually! When he glimpsed the woman Bathsheba bathing, he was so possessed by lust for her that he tore her from her husband and sent the husband to the front lines of the war against the Philistines—committing murder and adultery under the influence of the same lustful spirit.

The story of what happened in those times is so fascinating. Every so often some writer or movie producer discovers this and produces a best-selling book or top-box-office motion picture; I'm just waiting for television to discover some of the absorbing material in the Old Testament and come out with another fascinating TV series. The conflict is real—not just between nations and people—but inside the hearts of individuals like David. See how poorly this man, in so many ways "a man after God's heart," directed his family. David's children seemed to get away with anything!

David's son Amnon, possessed by rebellion and lust, raped and dishonored his own sister Tamar. Then their brother Absalom took revenge into his own hands. But he too became so rebellious that he not only killed Amnon but tried to take the kingdom away from his father David, beginning the chaos and unrest that split the kingdom in two and finally ended in the decay and fall of both halves.

I've just been referring to the two Books of Samuel in the Old

Testament. Read on into the Books of Kings and you get that story of the increasing unbelief and wickedness in the two kingdoms. One of the high points in the drama was that low point in evil when the wicked king and queen, Ahab and Jezebel, teamed up with the heathen god Baal against those who believed in the Lord. The prophets of Baal multiplied until there were hundreds of them.

But the Bible shows (in chapters 16 to 19 of 1 Kings) that when evil was at it its strongest, God produced unusual displays of power. Elijah had to flee into the wilderness and there ravens brought him food. He challanged the four hundred and fifty prophets of Baal to a spiritual duel and they couldn't equal what God did. They leaped and shouted and cut themselves until their blood flowed, but Baal was silent. Then Elijah prayed just once to the Lord God of Israel, and fire seared down from the heavens and burned up the water-soaked sacrifice on Elijah's altar!

Through all this Elijah and his successor Elisha showed what would today be called psychic powers. The son of King Ahab heard that Elisha knew the words whispered in the king's bedroom (2 Kings 6:12). Surrounded by the king's forces, Elisha was protected by the angels and chariots of the invisible hosts of God (2 Kings 6:15ff.). Elisha knew the future (2 Kings 7:1). When evil power hits hardest, God makes His power most evident. He did it then, He did it when Jesus was on earth, and He will do it again at the end of this age as everything shapes up for His return.

If you know the Bible, you may be thinking that you know the history I've just been referring to. But do you know what was behind the decline and fall of the people of God? It's made remarkably clear in one case. In 1 Kings 22 you learn of a man named Micaiah who knew what it meant to be unpopular. He never preached what people wanted to hear. He always said what the Lord gave him to say. When Micaiah refused to preach the kind of patriotic sermons the king demanded, he was thrown into prison. All the other preachers said exactly what the king wanted to hear. Which was right: Micaiah or the majority? The Bible says it was Micaiah. How do you explain the clear consensus of the other prophets? The Bible says a lying spirit was in their mouths (v. 23).

You see, the Bible takes us back behind the scenes every once in a while. The history of Israel is not just the story of men and women and wars and defeats and victories. It's really an invisible struggle between God and His angels against Satan and his demons. On one side are the Lord and all the hosts of heaven. On the other are the demons that try their best to win control of the hearts and minds of humans, and turn them against God. Once in a great while the veil drops and we see the real conflict. Especially today it becomes clear what is going on. The power of God is sweeping through the world! And at the same time demonic power is manifesting itself in so many ways. It will keep on that way until the end.

10

Jesus and the Invisible World

Whenever I preach, I'm conscious of two others on the platform beside me. I know Jesus is there with me. He stands at my side, yearning for those who don't know Him to turn to Him and find His love. He gives me words to tell to each new audience what He has done in my life, and how much He can do for anyone else. When I finish speaking and men and women and young people start coming forward to take a new stand for God, I can sense His Spirit pleading with them, drawing them toward His loving arms.

But I know that Satan is there too. I know he has tried his best to keep various individuals from coming to the meeting. Whenever there's a disruption I can feel his attempts to create disorder and keep people from listening to the message of God. I sense his attempt to draw a veil over my listeners' hearts, to keep them from hearing what God wants them to know, to distract their thoughts, to prevent them from making a definite decision for Christ. I know that the struggle between Satan and Jesus is always taking place, and will never end until this age itself ends and God and Jesus are finally completely victorious.

You can see that struggle between the two invisible armies all through the gospels. An angel appeared to Mary to announce that Jesus was going to be born (Luke 1:26–38) and an angel appeared to Joseph to confirm His virgin birth (Matthew 1:18–24). Angels were glimpsed again and again during His birth and childhood, according to the first two chapters of both Matthew and Luke. When He grew up and was tempted, angels came to help Him (Matthew 4:11). When He struggled in Gethsemane in prayer, an angel came to bring Him strength (Luke 22:43). When He was arrested He said He could summon multitudes of angels to help Him if He so desired (Matthew 26:53). And angels rolled the stone away from His grave (Matthew 28:2).

Ask the average person what Jesus did and he's likely to say, "He set a good example." He may add, "Jesus also taught about God." He may possibly also say, "He healed sick people." What many people don't know is that Jesus also spent much of His time casting out evil spirits.

The first opposition to Jesus mentioned by Mark was from a man possessed by an unclean spirit (1:23). Early in His ministry He cast out many demons (Mark 1:34; 3:11). And He continued this work of deliverance all through His life.

No wonder the prince of the demons, Satan, tried at the very beginning to destroy Him, first by the sword of Herod (Matthew 2:16) and then by direct temptation (4:1–11). If he had persuaded Jesus to turn against His Father and sin, what a great victory it would have been for hell! But Jesus stood every test.

All through Jesus' life you can see Satan attacking Jesus through the religious leaders who hated Him, and how they twisted His words and tried to get Him put to death, using Satan's oldest weapons, *deceit* and *destruction*. When that didn't work, Satan tried to ruin Jesus by influencing His own disciples. Only about one minute after Peter made that great confession of faith, "Thou art the Christ, the Son of the living God," he was trying so hard to keep Jesus from going to the cross that He called him Satan (Matthew 16:23). Jesus recognized that His blood would have to wash away the sin of the world, and knew that any suggestion that bypasses the cross has to be from Satan.

Jesus knew that through His death the prince of this world would be driven out (John 12:31). But Satan didn't. The two big activities of Satan are lying and killing. So the devil put the idea into the mind of Judas to betray Him (John 13:2), and when Judas made the final decision to do this—right at the Last Supper, as he took the bread from the hand of Jesus—Satan entered into him (John 13:27). There have been many cases of demon possession. With Judas Iscariot it was a definite case of possession by Satan himself.

Go on into the Book of Acts and you see exactly the same conflict continuing. Probably the most famous liar in the Bible was Ananias, who told the Apostles he was bringing them all the money he got for his property while he had secretly kept part of it for himself. The Apostle Peter instantly recognized what had happened: ". . . how was it that Satan so possessed your mind?" (Acts 5:3 New English Bible). A member of the church who gives a tremendous amount is not immune from Satan's domination! By striking at members of the church he strikes at the church's Head, Jesus.

In the eighth chapter of Acts we come across one of the early practitioners of occult arts. Simon of Samaria used some kind of sorcery to bewitch people; he must have made them believe his magic could give them supernatural powers—people called him "the great power of God" (v. 10). When Philip came there with the gospel, many believed for the first time in Christ, and Simon was among them. But when he saw the Holy Spirit coming upon the converts, he was so fascinated that he tried to bribe the Apostles to give him the power to bestow the Spirit. At this the Apostle Peter denounced Simon's wickedness and Simon, realizing the sin of trying to buy a gift of God, repented and begged Peter to pray for him.

Apparently Simon thought money could buy anything. He had been so deeply mixed up in the occult that it was a slow process to get his mind straightened out and realize the complete difference between magic powers and the total power of God. At first the superior power of the gospel blew Simon's mind. Then, falling back into occult ways of thought, he tried to *buy* what you can only *accept as a gift*. That's the very heart of the occult: to try to get supernatural help by *doing* something. The only kind of help you get that way is Satan's help. Fortunately, Simon came to realize that, and the danger of imagining he could control the Spirit of God. The Spirit has to control us!

Some of the Christian messengers contacted another sorcerer on the island of Cyprus. Elymas may well have made his living by selling the supernatural. When Paul and others started talking to the governor about Christ, Elymas sensed the threat to his way of life and spoke against the Christians. At that Paul, filled with the Holy Spirit, said to Elymas, ". . . thou child of the devil . . . thou shalt be blind, not seeing the sun for a season . . ." (Acts 13:10, 11). Immediately the sorcerer lost his sight, and the governor, astonished, believed in the Lord.

In Greece, Paul and his friends came across a slave girl with the spirit of divination, fortune telling. When she saw the Christians she knew who they were: "These men are servants of the most high God . . ." (Acts 16:17). What she said was true—but she knew it by occult power, and it interfered with the Christians' witness. So, in the name of Jesus, Paul commanded the spirit to come out of the girl, and it departed.

At the city of Ephesus Paul witnessed, healed the sick, and cast out evil spirits. There were seven brothers there who practiced magic. When they saw what Paul was doing, they tried using the name of Jesus to cast the spirit out of a possessed man. But the evil spirit said, ". . . Jesus I know, and Paul I know; but who are ye?" (Acts 19:15). Then the man flew at the seven brothers, tore off their clothes, and battered them so hard they had to run to get away from him. It is dangerous as well as wicked to use the name of God or Jesus without committing yourself to Him.

There were quite a number of occultists at Ephesus. Many of them were converted when Paul talked to them. They confessed that they had been dealing in things no one should touch. Then they burned their expensive books of magic—books worth thousands of dollars!

Today, when so many people are experimenting in so many phases of the occult, it is important to realize that no Christian can have anything to do with fortune telling, astrology, spiritualism, witchcraft, or any of the other traps Satan is setting. A high-school girl who is one of the Jesus People saw all the occult books her father was reading and told him, "Dad, you ought to burn those." She was right.

For there can never be anything in common between Christ and

Satan. Christ is Life, Satan is the destroyer and murderer. Christ is Truth, Satan is a liar and deceiver. God is Love, Satan is hatred personified.

One of the most alarming movements of the twentieth century is the Process Church of the Final Judgement. Its members (who work hard in Chicago and Boston and New York and Toronto and on a good many college campuses to get young people into its organization) teach an abominable doctrine: that Christ and Satan are both parts of God. They are both parts of human personality, too, say these people; "God is all things" and "love means a universal, all-embracing, all-forgiving acceptance and conciliation." "Through Love, Christ and Satan have destroyed their enmity and come together." These statements from the literature of the Process Church show how far-removed that organization is from any church of Christ.

A pamphlet from the Process Church recently contained on the same page prayers to Jesus, Lucifer, and Satan. The prayer to Satan ended, "Teach me to fear not, to know you Great Lord!"

May God keep everyone who reads this book from knowing the deceiver and destroyer of souls.

11

Questions I'm Most Often Asked

One evening a high-school psychology teacher asked me to meet with some students to talk about the occult. After I had shared some of the experiences I've related in this book, the students fired questions at me. Many of their questions are the same ones I'm asked over and over as I travel to different parts of the country.

A small teen-age girl with her red hair in braids asked, "But how do you explain those things? You don't really believe in demons, do you?"

That question gave me a chance to talk about the invisible world that so many people don't believe in because they can't see it. These are some of the points I discussed:

Some people say it's too simple to believe in God and the Bible. Actually, it's the other way around. Anyone who thinks that this visible world is everything, is ignoring the most important things. No one can see love or truth, or loyalty or patriotism or personality or spirit. For that matter, no one can see electricity! But you can feel its power, and if you want to, you can feel the power of God.

So it doesn't make sense to believe only in what you can see. There is much more to the world than what can be measured in a laboratory. The Bible says *yes,* there is a material world of things you can see with your eyes and feel with your five senses, but there is also a spiritual world you feel with the heart. This world I know because God reached down and picked me up when I was without hope, and let me know He loved me.

The first great fact in this spiritual world is God. How can something come out of nothing? How could there be a world unless God made it? The Bible says that in the beginning God created the heavens and the earth, and this explains the universe! God is Spirit, and like a wonderful Father He loves us and longs for us to be the best possible kind of persons, to love Him and each other. Many people see that love and caring are important, but it is God who puts that longing within us and shows us how to love in a world of hate.

The most important way God has shown this is in sending His Son to live on earth as a human being, to suffer, to be hurt and insulted and arrested and to die. Jesus shows that it is possible to love imperfect people, bad people, even enemies. And He makes it possible to do this, for He died for our sins and puts His life inside us so we are born a second time to become like Him.

When Jesus puts His life in us, He wants to seal this by giving us His Holy Spirit. The Spirit of God within us makes it a delight and a joy to do what God wants, to love what He loves and to witness to other people about Christ. So our spirits are strengthened and encouraged by the Holy Spirit, who is like the sap that brings life and growth to the branches of a tree or vine.

As the Bible shows, all of us are spirits first and bodies second. And God has whole armies of servants, usually called angels or spirits. But the Bible also explains that there is an evil side to the spiritual world. The evil world is made up of evil spirits, headed by their own leader, Satan. Satan is usually called the devil and his agents are known as demons. The interaction between humans and these — God, His messengers, the devil, and his demonic forces — gives the best explanation of what happens in so many lives.

At that point a very tall young man with bushy sideburns and a suede jacket asked, "But where did Satan and the demons come from?"

There are a lot of things we don't know, but in the beginning God created everything there is. All the demons must have been good angels once, for everything God makes is good. Still, God gives humans the power of choice and freedom of will. He must do the same thing with the spirits we call angels and demons. Apparently there came a time when Lucifer decided he would become like God or overthrow Him, and many angels joined in the attempt. Of course they could not succeed, so they were banished from heaven.

So now there are two spiritual orders — the kingdom of darkness and the Kingdom of God. The order of evil and darkness is very attractive today to a lot of people. The important thing is to know we're on the side of the order of light and justice and goodness and love, and that's the new order of God and Christ.

A chubby young fellow with thick glasses said, "But do you think demons can attack people?"

I do because I have seen it. Once the devil and his angels were thrown out of heaven, they tried to get back at God by getting the earth God created and the human beings God planned to have dominion over, under their own control.

Satan and the demons want bodies. Satan went into the body of a serpent to tempt Adam and Eve. When they can, the demons go into the bodies of people. I have seen their possession of people, and I know their attacks. They have no business on this earth. They are aliens from beyond this world who try their hardest to control us and take us with them to hell.

Those invisible spirits don't like to be exposed. Most of the time they do very well not letting anyone know they are around. But when Jesus came, the veil was drawn back and they could be seen in His great light, trying to organize people against Him, lurking in an evil heart here, a deranged mind there. The demons knew Jesus and trembled at His power.

Today, as the time draws closer when He may come back, once more the evil spirits seem to be exposing themselves. They will stop at nothing to try to get whoever they can under their power. This is what is behind the whole occult revival you see spreading so fast today.

The demons glitter and fascinate, but they don't want you to know what they are really up to. So they use all these tricks and disguises.

To illustrate that I told the young people a story I had just heard from a New Jersey friend of mine. My friend's daughter had spent a college term in Jamaica, and there she got acquainted with a young native of that island named Tim.

From his earliest years Tim had been exposed to the *obeah* (witchcraft) you find in so much of the Caribbean. One night he found a blue bottle under a banana tree on his father's plantation. He knew that it had been put there to work a curse on his father's bananas and destroy his crops, so he threw the bottle over the fence that surrounded the banana grove. As he ran toward home he saw red eyes glaring at him from the shadows.

One night when Tim was six years old he felt someone in his room where he still slept in an old-fashioned trundle bed. At first Tim thought his mother had come into the room. Then he became conscious of a light in the room and of someone standing by his bed. He felt as though this person was smiling at him. Finally the light faded and the presence seemed to go away.

"Mother," Tim called to his mother across the hall, "were you in here?"

Tim's mother came quickly to the door. "No, son," she said. "Why do you ask?"

"Oh, I thought someone was in here," said the little boy. "It seemed like someone came in and looked at me."

"It must have been an angel," Tim's mother told him.

When Tim was eight he was visited again. This time—and frequently afterward—several persons seemed to come to him at odd times. Each time the boy felt that he was among friends.

Tim was a lonely boy. The youngest of three boys, he longed to play with his brothers but with the cruelty children often practice unconsciously, they usually left Little Brother out of their activities. Who wanted to be bothered looking after the baby of the family?

As a result, Tim often played by himself. He started looking in a mirror, imagining the person he saw was another self, talking with his imaginary alter ego. Sometimes the other self took on a strange unexpected reality.

When Tim started playing with a Ouija board, the "friends" and the imaginary self began delivering strange messages. Tim found himself communicating with beings who lured him into exciting experiments.

He found that he could summon what appeared to be invisible but powerful spirits. They made uncanny predictions, seemed to guard him from danger.

Four of Tim's school friends made plans to pick him up for a drive to Montego Bay. When they arrived at his home in a car, they were stupefied at his sudden refusal to go with them. "I just don't feel like it," was his only explanation. As they drove angrily away without him, Tim thought to himself: *How can I tell them? Would they believe me if I told them that my spirit friends warned me not to go?*

The next day Tim was not nearly as surprised as his parents when the news came that all four friends were in the hospital. As they had neared Montego Bay, a truck coming around a curve on their side of the road sideswiped their car and sent it off the road into a fence.

Tim went deeper and deeper into occult arts. One day he invoked a spirit that came to him by the name of Mephistopheles. Promising unusual powers, Mephistopheles suggested that Tim perform strange tasks that led him ever farther into a demonic world. Soon Tim dipped into astrology and became fascinated at how his life seemed to have been shaped by the conjunction of the planets at his birth. At a Florida university he added to the subjects he was taking a course in astrological psychology. Tim also studied Buddhism. Buddha's doctrines of seeking unity with the divine through meditation strongly appealed to him. He was especially impressed that Buddha was teaching this hundreds of years before Jesus was born.

It all added up to a neat, attractive package: guidance, protection from danger, at-one-ness with the Infinite.

Then Tim met Nancy, my friend's daughter, while she was taking her winter college term in Jamaica. Nancy listened carefully to everything Tim told her so enthusiastically about his occult adventures. Then she told him what Jesus Christ had done for her. She knew something about spirits, she said. She herself had often been obsessed with a feeling of depression and despondency, and she had been led on occasion to command an evil spirit to leave a person, in the name of Jesus.

"But these aren't evil spirits," Tim protested hotly. "Through Buddhism I'm close to God."

"Jesus is the way to God," said Nancy. "There is no other way. He said, 'I am the way, the truth, and the life: no man cometh unto the Father, but by me'" (John 14:6).

Tim seethed when Nancy talked like that about Christ. He felt that she was putting down the whole beautiful world he had created. The name of Jesus especially angered him. But something about this girl kept him talking to her. When she told him very calmly that she was simply letting God speak through her, Tim knew deep in his heart that she was speaking the truth. Her words burned into his consciousness with great conviction.

The spirits began bothering him at night. Sometimes he would hear dogs barking nearby as he felt their presence. He told Nancy, "I've told the spirits to go away and not come back."

"They will come back," said Nancy. They did.

One night soon afterward Nancy awoke in her dormitory room about 3 A.M. Strange noises sounded throughout the dormitory—noises she had never heard before for it was usually very quiet in the dorm at night. Nancy was aware of a wicked presence nearby. Fear gripped her for several nights as the same sequence was repeated.

One evening as Nancy talked with Tim, continuing their previous conversations, she became aware of an alien spirit presence. The apartment door suddenly slammed shut. Tim seemed nervous but tried to cover it by talking, jumping from one topic to another. He knew that a spirit had entered the room and hoped Nancy wouldn't notice it.

Nancy sensed the presence but this time she felt no fear. Instead, although she felt weak within herself, she sought help from God and felt powerful rushes of strength from His Spirit. To each of Tim's arguments against Christ's claims she found an answer.

The dark, heavy presence seemed to grow. A curtain over the window billowed out—although the window was shut. A little later the cover of Tim's record player popped open.

Tim said, "There is a spirit in the room."

"I know," said Nancy.

"Start praying," Tim asked.

Nancy said a simple prayer: In the name of Jesus she told the spirit to leave—and she felt it go.

Soon afterward Tim knelt down and renounced the spirits with whom he had dealt for so long. Later he said, "I felt compelled by the Spirit of God to do this."

When he had turned his life over to Jesus Christ, Tim felt completely exhausted. But that night he rested in a wonderful sense of peace.

The next morning he and Nancy talked again. Nancy reminded Tim of Jesus' parable of the spirit who left a man, only to return to the empty place later with seven more evil spirits. "The way to keep that from happening," she said, "is to be filled with the Holy Spirit."

That morning Tim knelt again and asked the Holy Spirit to fill his life. He rose up filled with the joy of His baptism.

Now that he had made a clean commitment, Tim found that he had lost something. He was conscious that his occult powers were largely gone, along with the guidance and protection he used to have.

The evil ones had not forgotten what had happened. One morning about six weeks later Tim was feeling proud of his spiritual achievements as he rode his bicycle through the little college town. As he came to a stop sign at an intersection, his hands and feet froze. He could not stop. He shot at about 25 miles an hour into the main thoroughfare.

There was only one car on the street, but it was headed directly for Tim.

"God, help me!" Tim silently pleaded, aware of his helplessness. Some-how—no one can explain how—there was no collision.

So Tim is learning about the new kind of protection and guidance of the Holy Spirit.

When my friend told me this, Tim had recently visited his home. On one of his first nights there, my friend's wife had a terrifying nightmare. She dreamed that the table and chairs in the dining room were moving about independently, grotesquely, as though pushed by invisible hands. Then the sofa and the lamps in the next room began to writhe and crawl, and made obscene motions. It seemed that the house was in demonic hands, and she awoke in more terror than she had ever experienced in her life.

The same night Tim, sleeping in a room nearby, woke up with the feeling that something was clawing at the window. He got the horrifying impression that a being of tremendous evil powers was trying to get into his room. When he told the family about it, he said, "I've only been afraid one other time in my life, but last night I was *scared.*"

I was going to end this chapter here, but now I must add a post-script. My New Jersey friend tells me that Tim's health has just been severely attacked. In spite of the doctors' pessimistic reports, Tim has a radiant faith in Jesus. He knows the power of the devil—knows it too well to ever turn back from the light and love of Christ.

12

Satan's Computer Programs

A little while ago a business friend in Illinois was showing me his computer. He said, "This will tell me almost anything I want to know about my customers. It's programed to send our Christmas catalog to everyone who bought ten dollars or more from us within the past year. And I use it for personalized computer letters."

"Your computer writes letters?" I asked.

"Almost," my friend said. "It will sort out any information we want about people, say for instance, all the families on our lists with small children. Then we can use it to send each family a letter pitching our children's clothing. Each letter will repeat the customer's name three times and mention the town he lives in and the street he lives on. It's very effective salesmanship."

I've been thinking about the way Satan operates. If he doesn't have a computer, he has something better to increase his business. He knows all the ways to appeal to the worst in us and get us hooked on his devilish ways of life!

With some people he uses fortune-telling through palm-reading. I had to stay one night in a hotel in Miami and while I was waiting in the lobby I heard someone talking very enthusiastically behind a potted palm tree. When I walked around behind it I saw an easel with a sign on it:

MADAME FLORESSA
PALMISTRY
PERSONAL COUNSELING
APPOINTMENTS MUST BE MADE IN ADVANCE

Near the sign a middle-aged woman with a dark turban on her head was holding the hand of a girl who looked about twenty. "This summer," I heard her saying, "you will meet a man who will offer you unusual opportunities. He will become one of the most important men in your life. At first you may think this is just another date, but you will be mistaken.

"Now I see a crisis coming within the next two years. You will have to decide. . . ."

At that point the person I was waiting for came along and I never found out what the crisis was all about — but I could see Madame Floressa's appeal to that girl. She was telling her all the things most girls daydream about until the right man comes into their lives.

With others it's tarot cards. After seeing the motion picture *The Magus,* dealing with bizarre occult rites based on tarot, Gary Wilburn became fascinated with those strange cards which have been used by so many people to predict the future. When he asked the cards to reveal the future of himself and some friends, he was amazed at how accurate the predictions were.

For one friend, the future laid out by the tarot cards seemed unusually depressing, so he repeated it. Result: the same basic prediction as before, but even clearer. When Gary's friend told him she had received the same prediction from another tarot reader and from a palmist, he was alarmed. When the predictions all came true within a year, Gary resolved never to use the cards again. Now serving a church in California, Gary Wilburn tells this incident in his fine book *The Fortune Sellers.*

For some people Ouija is one of the means Satan uses to forge a fascination with the occult. This innocent-looking game (which means *Yes-Yes* in French and German) can sometimes be found nowadays in Christian homes and even churches. Yet many have testified that it is the entering wedge for demonic oppression!

A girl interviewed at a drug-abuse center in California said, "Before I came to the center I wasn't involved in witchcraft. My friends were just beginning to get interested in sort of adverse things — things I really couldn't go along with because they seemed to be getting into such a weird bit — like they were getting so heavily into drugs that when drugs didn't satisfy them, that's when they were exposed to witchcraft." (Quoted in *The Jesus People Speak Out!* compiled by Ruben Ortega and published by Pyramid Books.) A college student in Indiana said: "Demon possession starts in lots of ways. I think it often begins with drugs or meditation because when you're opening your mind, it's very easy for the demons to get in."

Drugs, yes. Most Christians would agree that the devil could use drugs to get people into his control. But *meditation?*

A recent issue of a magazine for young people featured a long story about a boy who invoked Satan and found himself unable to keep from committing a series of ritual murders. In the same magazine was an article about transcendental meditation. It repeated testimonials from high-school and college students about how wonderful they felt and how their school work had improved since they began practicing this form of meditation. Some of the students said they got such good feelings from it that they no longer used drugs.

After this enthusiastic sales pitch for transcendental meditation, the magazine listed places where classes are held, and for those not near enough to attend the classes it gave an address from which lessons could be bought by mail.

That makes me angry. If the same magazine listed the addresses of churches where young people could hear the liberating Gospel of Christ, you can imagine how many protests there would be. But who raises a word of protest when youth are urged to try a new religion?

For that's what transcendental meditation is. It's an attempt to find peace and God without the only bridge to God, Jesus, so it opens the mind to demonic suggestions that may eventually lead to ruin. Francis Schaeffer says of transcendental mysticism: "Some of it is straight Eastern thinking, some an amazing mixture of mysticism and the occult, and some is completely demonic." (From *The*

New Super-Spirituality by Francis A. Schaeffer and published by Inter-Varsity Press.)

Max Gunther, a Connecticut writer who has done quite a bit of research into the occult, once talked with a man named Al Manning about how to get acquainted with your familiar spirit. Manning recommended emptying the mind so the spirit can make itself known to the consciousness. The emphasis of transcendental meditation on avoiding conscious thought can lead to exactly such results — and to demon possession.

One of the most popular of all the routes to the occult is astrology. There's hardly a newspaper today without a daily horoscope. At one newsstand where paperbacks were sold I counted forty-eight books and seventeen magazines — each with a different title — on astrology. Now you can even buy forecasts that are supposed to be run up by computers. One of the first things many strangers ask when they meet is "What's your birth sign?"

I would be the last person to say there is no truth in astrology. There seems to be increasing evidence that the phases of the moon are connected somehow with such things as the level of crime and the birth rate, and if the moon can affect human beings, maybe the planets do. But every part of the occult world has a grain of truth mixed with a ton of falsehood and a hundred tons of demonic attraction, designed to get you out of God's control and into Satan's.

So if you get interested in astrology, you may very well find enough truth in it to lead you ever deeper into its spell. But let me mention some of its tricks and deceptions. For one thing, most of the astrological predictions I see are made in such vague language — like that of most so-called prophets today — that they might fit almost anything that happens. But when they get down to specifics, how wrong they can be!

A friend of mine who writes for a living told me that he gets a kick out of reading astrological predictions *after* a day's work instead of before. He said, "If you read Carroll Righter in the morning and he says 'You are highly magnetic today,' and if you're as suggestible as most people, you'll probably go around feeling magnetic all day and think Righter was right. But if you read the astrological column after the day is over, you can get a lot of chuckles. Last Monday I got several terrific ideas for a book I'm writing. That night I looked up what Jeane Dixon wrote for my horoscope and it said: 'Simple explanations open official doors for you. No detail is small enough to be skipped.' Carroll Righter said: 'Pay bills and improve credit. Avoid one who argues.'

"Neither column said anything whatever about the great ideas I got that day. No doors opened or closed and I didn't come across anyone who argues. Both astrologers rang up complete misses. What drivel!"

In the middle of 1972 I picked up a paperback *Astrological Guide to the Presidential Candidates* with these words on the cover: WHO WILL BE THE NEXT PRESIDENT? The book was written by Sybil Leek and published by Ace Books. Would you like to know who this well-publicized witch picked in 1971 for the winner in the 1972 election? Her book had a lot of the typical beating-around-the-bush, but she did say that gradually most of the hopefuls would be eliminated (correct) and that as a result "we shall get down to the true issue of Muskie-Kennedy-Humphrey versus Nixon-Connally." Not a bad guess in 1971!

What Sybil says about Richard Nixon is not very nice. And the planets are "bound to reflect on Mr. Nixon's chances of being a serious candidate in this Presidential year." If President Nixon wasn't a serious candidate in 1972, I'd like to know who was. But *if* Nixon should run, Sybil predicted, "I am going to go out on the limb and give Mr. Connally the chance to be the favorite running mate."

What about those Democratic contenders? Well, said Sybil, between the planets and Lindsay and Muskie, George McGovern hardly had a chance to be nominated. Who did? In Sybil's own words, "the man with the greatest astrological potential for becoming the President of the United States by popular vote of the people in 1972" was none other than Senator Harold E. Hughes. Are you surprised? The stars must have been surprised too when Hughes wasn't even nominated!

Satan appeals to some people through lust. Professor Owen Rachleff, who does not believe in the occult even though he teaches a university course in it, says of witchcraft groups: "I am inclined to believe that many of the contemporary cults are more or less orgy clubs cloaked in ritualism which gives them some amount of propriety." (Quoted in *Voodoo, Devils, and the New Invisible World* by Daniel Cohen and published by Dodd, Mead & Company.) Undoubtedly it is the prospect of uninhibited sex that attracts many people to various occult organizations and practices.

There are so many roads to Satanic domination! I don't have room to list them all. But don't think that the occult is Satan's only tool. He can use practically *anything* to tempt you in his direction—even religion. Don't forget that it was the religious experts in Jesus' day that He called the children of the devil. Look that up in the eighth chapter of John.

Yes, Satan knows all the angles. I don't doubt that he knows more about each of us than we suspect, and he is ready with all kinds of personalized appeals, each one tailormade for our own weaknesses, to get us into his power. He has his own Bible and his own gospel.

Anton Szandor LaVey is a Californian who founded and heads what he calls the Church of Satan. At one of his church services a nude young woman reclines on an "altar" while semen and urine make up the "holy water" sprinkled on the "worshipers" from a dispenser in the form of a human phallus. Then the congregation hails the names of Moloch, Beelzebub, Satan, and other infernal deities.

LaVey has written something called *The Satanic Bible,* which was published by Avon Books in 1969. It contains such choice words of wisdom as these:

- He who turns the other cheek is a cowardly dog.

- Say unto thine heart, "I am mine own redeemer."

- Blessed are the ironhanded, for the unfit shall flee before them—Cursed are the poor in spirit, for they shall be spat upon.

- Satan represents all the so-called sins, as they all lead to physical, mental, or emotional gratification.

In his *Satanic Bible* LaVey glorifies Satan and ridicules Jesus and Jehovah. He extols the seven deadly sins and says it's only natural to indulge in lust, pride, greed, etc. He takes everything in the Bible and reverses it with hellish logic. He tells you among other things how to sell your soul, how to choose a human sacrifice, how to pray to the devil, how to perform satanic magic, and how to conjure lust and destruction of your enemies.

LaVey's book is not the only *Satanic Bible*. Each coven of witches is likely to have its own, made up of supposedly secret rites, invocations, and prayers. The deck of tarot cards has been called the devil's Bible in pictures. But all these devilish collections of infernal information offer a satanic gospel:

- a gospel of promises, promises that fail to satisfy.

- a gospel of magic powers that demand more and more, and produce less and less.

- a gospel of pseudoreligion—a hollow religious form with no substance.

Satan's gospel is a gospel of nothings. It denies the reality of God, of a Saviour, of heaven—and even denies that the devil and hell are real. It destroys true freedom and individualism and brotherhood and peace and love. It promises many of these things but provides only caricatures of them. Above all, it has no hope.

When the artist Michelangelo painted *The Last Judgment,* he pictured one man who is just beginning to realize he is in hell. His chin is sunk into his hand. His eyes are staring in the awful realization that he is lost forever. He knows now that there is no more hope for him anywhere, ever.

That is an accurate picture of the person who turns from the glorious Gospel of Christ to the garbled gospel of Satan.

13

Witchcraft Today

It's probably hard for most people to take witches seriously. From their childhood experiences they associate witchcraft with Halloween and black cats, broomsticks and pumpkins; or they pity witches, as they think about the Puritan witchcraft trials in New England.

The fact is that no witches were ever burned by the Puritans. Nineteen persons charged with witchcraft were hanged by them—but in Spain's Inquisition often one hundred were burned in a day. Whether they were Catholics or Protestants who did the killing, all Christians today confess that such violence was wrong.

All of which does not make witchcraft right. The fact that it was wrong to kill suspected witches does not mean it's right to pray to the devil. The pendulum of history swings from one extreme to another. I'm convinced that the execution of witches three centuries ago is no more dangerous an extreme than today's permissive acceptance of them as harmless dabblers in the occult.

It's true some of them seem harmless enough. It's hard to believe Sybil Leek would harm a mouse. Yet in her book *Cast Your Own Spell* published by Pinnacle Books she gives "a rather nasty little Italian spell to injure an enemy." The booklet *Everyday Witchcraft* claims to deal only in "white magic," which is supposed to be "good"—the opposite of "black magic," which is "not only unsavory, but dangerous." The same booklet tells you how "to bring bad luck," "to transfer an illness" (to someone you hate), "to physically torment an enemy." This is *good?*

Anything you say about witches, of course, can't tell the whole story. Some of them do try to deal in white magic only, some in black. Some meet in covens when the moon is full, some are solitary as hermits. Some witches are quite intellectual about restoring the Old Religion, as they call it, with all the proper rites and incantations; others are into witchcraft for sex and violence. Some wear black robes (or red or white) when doing their occult thing, while many prefer to work "skyclad"—nude—usually with others of both sexes. Some witches don't believe, they say, in actual evil spirits; many do.

But you don't need to eat a whole pie to know whether it's good or bad. Let me give you a taste or two of witchcraft and you can draw your own conclusions.

In the 1400s John V, Duke of Brittany, got complaints from dozens of parents that the Baron of Retz was stealing their children. Investigating, the Duke discovered that the Baron and his friends collected children to sacrifice in the Black Mass.

Like most of witchcraft, the Black Mass is hidden so deep in darkness that it's hard to tell where truth ends and illusion begins. However, some facts are certain about the way it was probably performed in medieval Europe. In a black-draped chapel, black candles adorned a black-shrouded altar. On the altar lay a nude woman, a cross between her breasts and a chalice between her thighs. With a host stolen from a Christian church, a defrocked priest said the Mass.

The high point of the ceremony was the sacrifice of an animal or a child.

The sacrifice was believed to release tremendous psychic power. The Baron of Retz must have wanted a lot of power, for he was executed after evidence was collected that he and his associates had murdered *more than a hundred children.*

In the seventeenth century a French girl named Françoise Montespan got a Parisian fortune-teller to have a Black Mass celebrated. The objective: to become the king's mistress. The magic worked. Louis XIV ditched a younger and—it is said—lovelier mistress for Madame de Montespan.

Then a new lovely caught Louis' eye, and back went the Madame to her fortune-telling friend. Another Black Mass was offered up to the evil powers. Once more Françoise had the king in her occult clutches.

But Louis had a far-roving eye, and his interest in other ladies of Paris sent Françoise scurrying back to the black chapel again and again for more masses.

Unfortunately for her, the parents of the children who were being sacrificed to keep Françoise in the king's arms objected. When they rioted, another investigation got under way and when Louis found out what had been going on, he sent Françoise off to a convent. Who wants to be tied to a hag who's been luring him with *magic?* The fortune-teller and her associates took the rap. Before they were put to death, they confessed that they had slaughtered 1,500 children in their diabolical rites.

So don't think all those witches brought to trial in the Middle Ages were innocent, sweet old ladies. Some of them may have been, but there is increasing evidence that witchcraft itself is and always has been a horrible mixture of paganism, blasphemy, and cruelty.

You say that's ancient history? Today there are probably more people practicing witchcraft than ever before in history. Some may try it for a lark, but witchcraft is no more a joke today than it ever was. It's dangerous and deadly.

In the last few years a group of American teen-agers was found nailing hamsters to a cross, two New York boys beat a baby to death and tied it to a cross. A California school teacher was murdered and her heart and lungs used in a sacrifice to the devil, and a New Jersey boy was thrown into a pond as part of a satanic ritual.

(I remember reading about Michael Newell in a New Jersey newspaper. He got interested in black magic because so many of his high-school friends were into it. This boy said the devil told him he would never die. He got two of his teen-age friends to tie his hands and feet and throw him into a pond, after he had held a service to the devil. Michael said that he would come back leading a legion of demons. He drowned.)

A minister from California told me of the strange things his daughter, in the third grade, said were going on in school. When she went into the girls' rest room at lunchtime she discovered about a dozen girls standing in a circle, holding hands and chanting something she didn't understand. Questioning her, the parents concluded that these grade-school children must have been holding some kind of seance or practicing some form of witchcraft.

Those who don't know any better may think God is dead, but no one today needs to ask whether the devil is real. He is alive and well and trying his best to destroy our children and young people!

Witchcraft has so many forms today that it's hard to keep track of them all. I have heard of a coven of female witches who outdo Women's Lib. Their whole purpose in life is to put down men — with a vengeance.

When these witches meet they call on evil spirits to harm or destroy various men. Then they put their "worship" into practice through the week.

Ann is a secretary. When she sees a construction gang working on a new building, she mentally concentrates on one of the men and silently chants a spell to make him fall. If the man does fall, Ann gleefully tells all about it at the next gathering of the coven.

Not to be outdone, Elspeth goes after her own man. While she is driving she notices a man in the car behind her trying to pass her. Elspeth speeds up, keeping the man's car behind hers until she is halfway up a hill. Then she slows down just as the man is going out of his mind with frustration — and just as a truck appears over the top of the hill. Elspeth nearly dies with joy when the stranger's car crashes head-on into the truck.

In the 1970s witchcraft is increasing all over the Western world. There are thousands of witches today in Italy, Switzerland, France, Germany, and many other countries. Witchcraft used to be illegal in England. Now the laws against it have been revoked and Britain's witches are coming into the open. But John Kerans, one member of Parliament, demanded new laws because, he said of the new flood of witchcraft, "A good deal of it is a cover for sexual orgies and other malpractices."

The Canadian magazine *Weekend* recently reported a witchcraft explosion in Canada. Newsman Emile Schurmacher says of witch-craft in Mexico: "Today the age-old practice of *brujeria* flourishes as never before in Mexican history, especially in border cities and towns where witches and witch doctors are being patronized more and more by Americans." (Quoted from *Witchcraft in America Today* published by Paperback Library.) Voodoo, macumba (spiritual-ism), and obeah (black magic) permeate every part of Brazil, the Caribbean, and Latin and South America.

And here in the United States thousands of witches keep multi-plying. If you think most of them are in California, you may not be keeping up with America's own witchcraft explosion. Martin Ebon says in *Witchcraft Today* (published by New American Library) that Manhattan in New York City probably has more witches per square mile than any other place in the United States.

Max Gunther got interested in the possible connection between witchcraft and the stock market. He asked the high priestess of one coven (who is also a secretary at an IBM office) what witchcraft meant to her. She said it gives power: "Not just some vague promise about going to heaven, but rewards you can actually see and touch and use in *this* world."

"Money, you mean?" asked Gunther.

"Yes. Money, love, sex—whatever you want."

Gunther attended a meeting of a Chicago coven that sometimes cast spells on the stock market. The eleven men and women present out of the thirteen who make up the coven were stark naked except for a few ornaments; witches in general believe that clothing interferes with their psychic power. The meeting began with chant-ing that Gunther later learned was the Lord's Prayer recited back-wards. A member explained that such things were supposed to liber-ate the members from "constricting religious traditions." Then the witches were flagellated by the high priest and priestess in turn.

Max Gunther described all this in an article in *True* magazine and a book entitled *Wall Street and Witchcraft,* published by Bernard Geis Associates. In the latter he comments: "In some covens, rituals such as this have direct sexual purposes as well. Many witches, male and female, are in the business mainly for the sex games involved. Witches who are sadomasochistically inclined will often whip each other at great length. In other covens they ritual-istically fondle each other's genitalia or unabashedly copulate while trying to raise demons and devils."

A kissing ritual and other ceremonies led to the attempt to raise the coven's familiar spirit, a demon of supposedly fantastic power, named Panandrio.

"Panandrio!" conjured the high priestess. "Come into this room!"

Everyone stared at a dark corner of the basement where some dried plants stood in an urn. There was a long period of silence. Then, Gunther says, *the dried plants moved*—and there were no drafts, nothing to make them stir. Nothing visible.

Later some of the witches told Gunther that Panandrio usually gave some sign of his presence; two of them said they had seen him appear as a smoky form.

Various petitions were put before the coven and its demon. One man asked for a rise in price of a certain stock. Another said he thought he had made a girl pregnant and asked for an abortion. The coven chanted over and over: "The baby must not be born." Later, Gunther was told, the man's girl friend underwent a spontaneous abortion.

Although some witches would deny it, there is a lot of sex in witchcraft. (Many witches say that Christianity is against sex, which is a lie. Christians are by no means antisex. We just don't want this beautiful gift of God degraded through promiscuity and demonic rituals.) In a typical coven, new members are initiated by "the five-fold kiss." When the initiate is female, the high priest leads her naked before the group, her hands tied behind her back, and flicks her with a whip. (If the new member is a male, the service is con-ducted by the priestess.) Then the initiate is kissed on the feet, the knees, the sex organs, the breasts, and the lips. Some covens have a "great rite" consisting of sexual intercourse. One witchcraft leader complained that too many applicants for membership wanted to get straight into the sex without waiting for the preparatory instruction. Too few of them realize that sex is the bait which will trap them in degradation, despair, and destruction.

Experts in the occult may say that in this chapter I've mixed up white witches and black witches, witchcraft and satanism. It's impossible to keep all this separate. Anton LaVey, the "satanic pope," says it's stupid to go halfway into witchcraft; he's all for having all witches admit they're into evil and leave it at that. And while Satan worship isn't necessarily traditional witchcraft, I notice that most witches seem on pretty familiar terms with Satan.

A librarian near New York said recently she's appalled at the number of teen-agers who keep asking for books on Satan, witchcraft, and the occult. When she asks them why they're interested, they tell her, "We're just fooling around—you know, seances and stuff like that."

A divorcee in Montana attached herself to a Christian woman and persuaded her to divorce her husband on no grounds except "mental cruelty." Those who know the divorcee say they believe she is possessed by Satan.

A filthy-looking young man wearing dark glasses and a cross hung upside down around his neck walked into a store in Tennessee. He told an inquirer that the cross was a perversion and that he worshipped the devil. Asked what he did about sin, he said, "Sin does not exist." Other things he said made no more sense. This man had with him a wife and two small children. From time to time the woman struck the two little ones ferociously for no reason anyone could see.

Do you wonder that I say Satan is on the loose?

14

The Tangled Mess

One of the first times I went fishing was in a little stream near my father's house with two of my older brothers. Soon after we got there, I remember, I was slowly pulling in my line when I felt a big tug.

"Hey!" I shouted to my brother Gene. "I've got a big one!"

"You'd better wait and see what you've got," said Gene. He realized before I did what had happened.

My fishing line had caught on a tangle of someone else's lost line at the bottom of the stream. Just when I thought that was it, I discovered that the tangle of fishing line was caught on an old shoe, and the shoe was tied somehow to the inner tube from a tire! When the whole mess, dripping with mud, came out of the water, my two brothers laughed so hard they rolled on the ground.

I think of that now in connection with the whole world of occult things. Witchcraft is heavily involved with astrology and evil spirits. Spiritualism leads on, very often, to the Eastern religions and to such ideas as reincarnation. All this is time and again mixed up with drugs and fortune-telling and all kinds of things God has expressly forbidden in the Bible.

For example, consider one of the most popular present-day "prophets," Jeane Dixon. When Jeane was a child of eight, her parents took her to a gypsy fortune-teller who read the lines in her hands and announced that she was a budding prophetess. The gypsy woman gave her a crystal ball in which the child looked to predict the gypsy might hurt herself with the pot in which she cooked. Soon afterward the woman burned her hands in scalding water from the pot.

Later Jeane Dixon was taught astrology by a priest, made more predictions from dreams and visions and cards. While she has a big reputation from such things as allegedly forecasting the death of John F. Kennedy, she has made misses as well as hits. When Lyndon B. Johnson was president, she went on record in print that he would be the 1968 nominee of the Democrats. This is the kind of prediction most people would have made, since a president in office is almost always nominated for a second term. But the events fooled everyone, including the prophetess in Washington, and the nominee turned out to be Hubert H. Humphrey.

The fact is that Jeane Dixon's prophecies relating to the presidents are not very good. She predicted that Richard Nixon would become president in 1960; Kennedy won the office instead. She predicted that Walter Reuther would seek the presidency in 1964; he didn't.

Mrs. Dixon also prophesied that China would go to war in 1968 and that Russia would be the first nation to put a human being on the moon. In 1966 she said the war in Viet Nam would come to an end in ninety days.

The day before Jacqueline Kennedy married Aristotle Onassis, Jeane Dixon's newspaper column carried the revelation that Mrs. Kennedy was not thinking of marriage. (Sources of information about Jeane Dixon come from *A Gift of Prophecy* by Ruth Montgomery, *The Occult Revolution* by Richard Woods, *Twentieth Century Prophet* by James Bjornstad, *Prophecy in Our Time* by Martin Ebon, and Jeane Dixon's *My Life and Prophecies* as told to Rene Noorbergen.)

Take another prophet with a large following today: Edgar Cayce. While this man, like Jeane Dixon, mixed a gloss of Christianity into his predictions, he too was strong on reincarnation. He taught that Jesus Christ was really a reincarnation of Adam, who had been in another incarnation the father of Zoroaster, the founder of the Persian religion of Zoroastrianism. As Adam, Jesus (according to Cayce) had plunged the whole world into sin and death. Through his various reincarnations, Adam worked his way up to Christhood.

The gospel of reincarnation is that we too do just this. Fail in this life? No sweat; you'll have a chance to come back to try for a better score next time around, until you reach the top!

Any Christian must be appalled at the idea that the Saviour ruined humanity in Eden, and had to *become* Christ through a series of pagan reincarnations; or that Jesus and Christ are two completely different concepts, as Cayce taught. Or that it is *not* appointed to men once to die, and after that the judgment, as the Bible teaches in Hebrews 9:27. Or that there is any other way of salvation than faith in Jesus Christ. But this is what you find in the teachings of Edgar Cayce. (Further information about Cayce may be found in Ebon's *Prophecy in Our Time,* Woods's *Occult Revolution,* and *Edgar Cayce's Story of Jesus* edited by Jeffrey Furst.)

Let me tell you about a young college student named Jim. While he was in San Francisco he fell in with some young people from the Haight-Ashbury and began to experiment with marihuana and other drugs. One evening he dropped some acid while he was at home and asked his father, a Protestant minister, to help him through his drug trip.

Jim felt he was going down a dark road that got blacker as he went. He was surrounded by shapes he couldn't quite make out, by unearthly sounds. He said, "This leads nowhere."

Jim's father asked him to turn around and come back, but the boy answered, "I'm afraid that's no good, Dad. I'm too far along." He felt everything getting blacker and more frightening. Finally he saw a light in his psychedelic trip and started toward it. Reaching it, he saw beautiful colors, heard harmonious sounds, and said: "I feel one with everything around. I'm One. The One. I'm God."

Later, at another university, Jim taped black friction tape to the ceiling above his bed and spent hours staring at it. One night his father noticed Jim's dilated pupils and concluded he must be on another drug trip.

This time Jim said haltingly he was seeing a column. Then he felt he was being sucked toward the column, into it: "I have become the column. . . . There is no difference between us. . . ."

Suddenly Jim felt himself falling into black emptiness. "Save me!" he begged. There was a long period of terror for both father and son. At last Jim saw a light, felt himself pulled toward it, rescued. He wrote on a piece of paper: HINDU ESCAPE COLUMN.

During the earlier drug session Jim's father recognized Jim's feeling, "I'm one with everything—I'm God," as the teaching of Buddhism.

Still later the father was shocked when the son took his own life. Bishop James Pike wrote a book about his experiences with his son Jim, entitling the book *The Other Side,* published by Doubleday and Co., Inc. In it he told how he contacted different mediums and became convinced that Jim was communicating with him from the spirit world. He asked Jim, "Have you heard anything over there about Jesus?"

"I haven't met him," Bishop Pike reported that Jim told him. "They talk about him—a mystic, a seer, yes, a seer. Oh, but, Dad, they don't talk about him as a saviour. As an example, you see?" A little later Jim said, "Don't you ever believe that God can be personalized. He is the Central Force and you all give your quota toward it."

Bishop James Pike, once an atheist, then a Roman Catholic, then an Episcopal bishop, then a rationalistic liberal who doubted the supernatural, finally a seeker of spiritualist mediums, is now dead.

But do you suppose this is another example of the tangled occult mess? In the case of his son Jim, it looks like a trip from spiritual emptiness to drugs to meditation to Buddhism and Hinduism to suicide. For his father the road led on to spiritualism and a sympathetic ear for Jim's alleged messages from beyond—and his denial of the Saviourhood of Christ and the personality of God. To me, it looks like another occult trap.

Charlie had quite a different upbringing. In some ways he grew up like a good many other American boys. He learned to play the guitar, got interested in psychology, hypnotism, science fiction, scientology. Scientology, a sort of new religion invented by a

science-fiction writer, appealed to Charlie because it blended together some kind of science with the promise of mental health and
happiness and personal power.

Charlie liked girls, cars, and money. Picking up all three here and
there brought him into prison a number of times during his teen
years. While he was in a federal prison in the state of Washington
Charlie got into more psychology, magic, and witchcraft.

When Charlie got out of prison he set up communal housekeeping
in the Haight-Ashbury section of San Francisco with a number of
flower children, mostly teen-age girls. Then dope and violence hit
the area, and Charlie and his girls moved out, warning people he
met that love and peace had fled the Haight.

Charlie, now in his thirties, bought a bus for his retinue and
headed south. In Los Angeles he befriended some people involved
in Satan worship and occult movies. Trying LSD, he thought he was
Jesus being crucified and from then on he and his girls used drugs a
lot — and Charlie decided he was both Jesus and Satan. On various
occasions, one of the girls said, "Charlie would put himself on a
cross. And a girl would kneel at the foot of the cross and he would
moan, cry out as though he was being crucified, and they also would
sacrifice animals and drink their blood as a fertility rite."

From time to time various members of Charlie's communal family
were arrested for taking dope or wandering about nude, but Charlie
and his friends had glib tongues and these days who wants to keep
anyone in jail? So usually the charges were quickly dropped and the
family grew, often living on the credit cards new members brought
with them. Some children of famous Hollywood personalities attached themselves to the group now and then. The living is easy
when anything goes and Papa and Mama give their adolescent
children credit cards.

Charlie liked California's motorcycle gangs — the Straight Satans,
the Jokers Out of Hell, the Satan Slaves. When a gang dropped by
he would offer them his girls. Some people say Charlie's group was
deeply influenced by the Process Church of the Last Judgement. in
which Satan is worshipped along with Jehovah, Lucifer, and Jesus,
although that organization denies this.

Charlie called his girls witches, and they seem to have tried acting like witches. In 1971 Charles Manson and three of his girls were convicted of the brutal murders of seven persons, including Sharon Tate, the actress whose husband, Roman Polanski, had directed the occult movie *Rosemary's Baby*.

What a tangle Charlie got himself and his friends into!

15

A Five-Point Program
For Parents

Recently a woman telephoned me from Oklahoma. "Dr. Cruz?" she said.

"I'm not a doctor," I said. "Call me Nicky."

"Very well, Nicky. I'm Jean Hawthorn. I have three children, and I was so disturbed today when my daughter in junior high brought home that book *Rosemary's Baby*. I think her English class is reading it. What can we parents do to protect our children from things like this?"

I don't remember all that I told Mrs. Hawthorn, but right here I want to say how important it is for parents to know what is happening today and to work to protect young people from one of Satan's worst mass onslaughts in centuries. Between drugs, pornography, and today's flood of occultism, our young people won't have a chance unless adults do all in their power to help them survive.

Here's the program I recommend to every Christian adult — and every concerned person:

1. ***Know what is happening.*** A few years ago young people faced the danger of a tremendous increase in exploitation from drugs. That threat will be with us for a long time, *but a far greater threat right now is the occult revival.* In this book I've tried to point

120

out some of the many dangers shaping up in this area. My biggest fear is that you will finish this book and go on to something else without doing anything about the occult menace. It's not enough to read and agree with what I've said here. You've got to learn the facts for yourself.

Take the books and magazines your children are reading. Are they wholesome or dangerous? You can't answer that question any more from the covers. The official magazine of a respected youth organization recently published an article about a house in England where ghosts are supposed to appear, illustrated with photographs of alleged ghosts peering out of a nearby tree. I don't want my children reading material like that, and you shouldn't either.

A bookstore I walked into had a whole rack filled with occult books. Books on witchcraft, spiritualism, reincarnation, fortune-telling, mediums, ESP, Eastern religions, and many other similar subjects. Books about Atlantis, Mu and Lemuria, astrology and yoga, voodoo and obeah, satanism, black magic, parapsychology, meditation, tarot cards, mysticism, spirit photography, dream interpretation, demonology, hypnotism, numerology, I Ching, UFOs, prophetic messages, poltergeists, alchemy, sorcery — it made my head swim to think about all the delusions being churned out and gobbled up by a spiritually-starved public.

Early in the 1970s there was an occult wave in movies and television with such dramas as *Rosemary's Baby, The Other,* and *The Possession of Joel Delaney,* and with ghosts, witches, and ESP getting a hearing on many popular programs. That wave has slackened a little as I write this, but I wouldn't be at all surprised to see a swami or guru sweep the country one of these days with a new television program.

Know what's going on in the schools your children attend. An English teacher in New Jersey drew the shades in her classroom and put out the lights while she told the class of her psychic experiences. "I think I'm a medium," she said as she told of the predictions she had made and the spirits she had contacted. In a psychology class in another school the students were given lessons in palm reading, pendulum divination, and the like.

A high school in Minnesota has a course in the supernatural in

which the students visit cemeteries, lie in coffins, watch crema-
tions, and imagine what it is like to be dead. Hundreds of other
schools and colleges today have official courses in witchcraft,
magic, and various phases of occult study. And recently the federal
government gave a grant to the International Meditation Society to
train one hundred high-school teachers to teach transcendental
meditation, which I've already discussed.

2. *Know the truth about the occult.* The people pushing meditation claim it gets students off drugs and into better attitudes. What if
it's the opening wedge for something worse than drugs? Heroin
was invented as a harmless substitute for opium. You know how
harmless that is. Today there's a worldwide turning inward. If God
doesn't fill the spiritual vacuum inside our young people, will Satan?

I urge parents to read what the Bible says about the occult. I've
already mentioned a number of passages on this subject. Here are
some more: Deuteronomy 18:9–22; Ezekiel 13:17–23; Isaiah
8:19–20; 47:9–13; Galatians 5:19–25; 2 Corinthians 11:14, 15;
Revelation 22:15. Study them and talk with your pastor about them.

3. *Warn your children about the dangers of the occult.* Debby
Berman wrote in the *Hollywood Free Paper,* an underground newspaper of the Jesus People, of how she read a book about spiritualism
during her junior year in high school. "I was fascinated," she said,
"by the strange powers I'd acquired and thought that if I got deeper
and deeper into the occult that I would finally discover what I
was looking for."

Debby soon got into automatic writing, in which a dozen spirits
possessed her. Then she began having blackouts and gaps in her
memory. Doctors said she had symptoms of epilepsy but could not
understand the reason.

Debby was assaulted mentally and physically by her spirit
acquaintances; visible bruises appeared on her skin. One night she
was attacked so furiously that she called on Jesus to help her. In
the darkness of her room Debby Berman saw Him drive away the
demons and felt His victorious presence. Now she is in Bible school
preparing to serve Him for the rest of her life.

Pat Boone's young daughter Laury once joined some friends at
school in chanting some witchcraft incantations. Although she did

not take this seriously, Pat and Shirley Boone say their daughter's personality changed in a frightening way until she was delivered through prayer.

Your young people should know what can happen to them in the satanic world of the occult. But don't open their minds to the demonic by overstimulating them with occult horror stories. Give them a *positive* view of the supernatural world. Let them see how great God is, what a wonderful Friend Jesus is, and how completely the Holy Spirit can guard anyone who lives in His power. Lead your children and young people to read the Bible for themselves and to absorb its balanced, spiritually healthful view of the invisible – as well as the visible – realm.

4. *Join others of like mind.* Get together with other Christians to discuss the spiritual and mental well-being of your children. The schools and the public media may listen politely to what one or two parents say, but they aren't likely to do anything about it unless a group of individuals band together and show some collective muscle. If organizations of power and influence face the power of a united citizenry, they will *listen* and do something.

Your church or Bible-study group may be the natural place to begin such a group. In any case, remember that if your faith doesn't lead to Christian action, it is lifeless (James 2:17).

5. *Find out what you can do to stop the occult onslaught.* You may need to protest. The federal government has ruled any form of Christian teaching or prayer out of the public schools. Every Christian parent should join in a protest that will be heard clear to Congress and the Supreme Court whenever other religions, whether in the form of witchcraft, spiritualism, Eastern meditation, fortune telling, spiritualism or whatever, are brought into the schools. If God has to go out of the schools, let's not sit by idly while Satan marches in.

Or you may need to join other Christians in new legislation. Certainly if the Bible can no longer be read in school, other religions must not be promoted there. In any case, you can make your voice heard loud and clear by your school board and all those with power to influence your children's minds and hearts.

As Christians, many of us don't like to get involved in politics.

It's usually dirty and disillusioning. But we can remember this question: "Who knoweth whether thou art come to the kingdom for such a time as this?" (Esther 4:14). And we should by all means remember the Jewish boy who was carried into a distant land to be educated in a pagan court. The court was filled with magicians and astrologers who were believed to have all kinds of deep wisdom. The Jewish youth was supposed to learn all this, but he refused to forget his God or the Scriptures. When crises came to the government, young Daniel knew the answers to questions that baffled the astrologers and magicians. And in due course he rose to a position of great power and influence in that government, pagan as it was. Read the whole story in the Book of Daniel.

If we don't get involved for Christ's sake, we'll have to let everything go to the devil.

16

Can a Christian Be Demon-Possessed?

The question above is one I'm asked most often of all. I didn't include it in the chapter I wrote about such questions because it deserves a whole chapter to itself.

To begin with, what *is* demon possession? When I think about that my mind goes back to a time many years ago in Puerto Rico. I was playing with some other little kids in a winding brook near our home in Las Piedras. After we had been fooling around in the creek for a couple of hours, a boy named Pablo grinned as he pointed at my right leg: "Hey, Nicky, what have you got on your leg?"

I looked down and there was what looked like a little black leaf near my ankle. But when I tried to brush it off I couldn't. It seemed to be growing out of my leg and it felt like leather. I yelled, "Eeeeeek!" and ran for home.

One look and Mama said, "Sit down, Nicky." She told me to hold still while she poured some salt on the black thing until it shriveled up and fell on the ground. "He is a bloodsucker," Mama said. "He did something to your leg so you will keep bleeding for a while, but you will be all right."

I thought I'd never stop bleeding where the bloodsucker had fastened to my leg, but after awhile the bleeding stopped and before long I forgot all about it.

How can you have an evil spirit inside you alongside your own spirit? What is it like? Well, it's something like having a bloodsucker fastened to you, sucking out your blood. You're thinking about other things when all of a sudden you feel something black and awful. You try to get rid of the horrible thing but there's no way unless you know how to do it.

Before Jesus came into my life and the evil spirits went out, I used to have terrible feelings of depression. Sometimes I would sit for hours at a time thinking the most lonely, despairing thoughts. Other times I'd be filled with hatred and violence.

Nandor Fodor is a psychoanalyst who has interviewed many people involved in the occult. One of them was a woman who struck him as unusually cruel and evil. She told Dr. Fodor that she had always been fascinated by the devil and had prayed to him even as a child. Eventually her parents became so frightened at what she was doing that they cast her out of their home. Fodor wrote about her in *The Haunted Mind: A Psychoanalyst Looks at the Supernatural* published by Helix Press.

This woman took into her own home a boy on whom she decided to experiment with hypnosis. Putting him into a trance in the center of a magic circle, she commanded him to go to hell and bring back the devil. The boy writhed in fear, although nothing happened.

But this woman would not give up. She put the boy into six hypnotic trances, each time repeating the command to bring the devil from hell. During the sixth and last one something happened which frightened her nearly out of her mind.

She saw a light appear in the magic circle. Two eyes she described as "big as eggs" became visible in the hazy light, eyes with a terrible penetrating gaze. The boy said in a deep voice, "The Evil that you conjured up speaks to you."

This woman said there was a bad smell in the room and the air felt icy cold. There was a choking breathing sound, and the woman became so frightened she shrieked, "Go back, never come again!"

The light and the evil presence disappeared, and the woman never dared try her experiment again. She felt that all her strength had been used up, and the boy said that an alien power tried several times to gain control of him.

Anyone may become demon-possessed—almost. Anyone but a Christian. *I do not believe it is possible for a person who trusts in Jesus Christ to be filled with an evil spirit, or dominated by one.*

I know that some Christian friends will not agree with me about this. I have even heard people talk about casting out "Presbyterian demons," "Methodist demons," etc. (I have friends in every denomination, and I think that is going too far!)

I know how strong and dangerous demons are. But I do not believe any demon can enter a dedicated Christian, because I know the power of God.

Let me say again that I know the power of Satan. He is evil personified; his whole nature is against everything God stands for. He is doing a lot in the world today that is obviously against Christ, and we should beware of all that. However, I think Christians often give the devil more credit than he deserves.

Many Christians have problems in special areas of their lives. Some smoke, realizing they shouldn't. Some are depressed more than they ought to be. Some have too many fears. Now, one of the common practices in some circles today is to label such hang-ups "demon of tobacco," "demon of depression," etc., and to cast them out in the name of Jesus.

I think that is often a cop-out. I believe it lets us blame too much of our own failures and laziness on the devil.

I know how Satan would like to trip us up with such sins. I know his hatred for Christ and His people; I know he can oppress even Christians with his power and malice. He can use the things of the world to tempt us and take our victory from us. Often the devil has put obstacles in my way in an attempt to keep me from victorious living. And if we allow ourselves to be weakened by those attempts, the devil can move right in and work on us with even more effect.

But the Lord works in our lives as we yield our wills to Him. The combination of *our will* with *His power* is what changes our lives into His image. As long as we are willing, He does the work. (See John 3:16; 1:12; Revelation 3:20.) When we fail, it's not a shortage of divine power but a failure of our own wills. James 1:14–16 explains it this way: "But every man is tempted, when he is drawn away of his own lust, and enticed. Then when lust hath conceived, it bringeth forth sin: and sin, when it is finished, bringeth forth death. Do not err, my beloved brethren."

So let's stop giving Satan the credit for our sins and hang-ups when our will is the deciding factor! Why try to put everything on Satan's shoulders?

Aware as I am of the power and malevolence of Satan, I am even more aware of the power and love of Jesus Christ, of the Cross that gave us life, and of the dynamic Holy Spirit in our lives. Scripture after Scripture comes to my mind as I think about the wonderful power of God.

"For the law of the Spirit of life in Christ Jesus hath made me *free* from the law of sin and death" (Romans 8:2)! "If God be for us, who can be against us? He that spared not his own Son, but delivered him up for us all, how shall he not with him also freely give us all things?" (Romans 8:31, 32). "For I am persuaded, that neither death, nor life, nor angels, nor principalities, nor powers, nor things present, nor things to come . . . shall be able to separate us from the love of God, which is in Christ Jesus our Lord" (Romans 8:38, 39).

In Ephesians Paul prayed that his readers might have the eyes of their understanding opened to know ". . . what is the exceeding greatness of his power to us-ward who believe, according to the working of his mighty power, which he wrought in Christ, when he raised him from the dead . . ." (1:19, 20). The same power of God that raised Jesus from the dead is available to every one of us today!

In the second chapter of Ephesians Paul reminds us that before we were Christians we lived ". . . according to the prince of the power of the air, that now worketh in the children of disobedience" (v. 2). But God has raised us up to sit in heavenly places with Christ, to do good works—not bad (vs. 4–6, 10). Again he prays that we will ". . . be strengthened with might by his Spirit in the inner man; That Christ may dwell in our hearts by faith . . ." (3:16, 17) and that we might be ". . . filled with all the fulness of God" (3:19). Then he praises the God who is ". . . able to do exceeding abundantly above all that we ask or think, according to the power that worketh in us" (3:20).

Other passages that make this so clear are Philippians 3:10; Colossians 1:19, 20; Hebrews 2:14–18; 4:14–16; 1 John 4:4 — and many, many more. The Word of God emphasizes *time and time again* the omnipotence of Christ. Why then should Christians be fearful that some demon or spirit is going to invade them when they are off guard? When we are living in the victory of Christ, *His* power fills us — *He* dwells within us in His fulness — and nothing can separate us from that power against our will (Romans 8:35–39)! We have received His Spirit of glorious liberty (Romans 8:21), and not the spirit of bondage to fear (Romans 8:15).

My Christian life is based on the liberty and freedom from fear I have with my Saviour. I don't need to walk in fear of demons or spirits, as long as I find victory in Jesus. If I begin to doubt and allow fears or temptations to get the best of me, then naturally Satan can use that to his advantage. But God's Word is so full of promises of victory, and Christ is so willing and able to keep those promises, I do not see any need to worry unnecessarily about Satan sneaking up and getting control of me!

We need the confidence of Philippians 1:6: "Being confident of this very thing, that he which hath begun a good work in you will perform it until the day of Jesus Christ." We need to be able to say: ". . . I know whom I have believed, and am persuaded that he is able to keep that which I have committed unto him against that day" (2 Timothy 1:12).

Those who teach that any Christian may be possessed by demons appeal to the story of Ananias and Sapphira in Acts 5. This man and his wife certainly seem to have been included among the believers who sold what they had and gave the money to the church (4:32–37). It is true that Peter told Ananias that Satan had filled his heart (5:3). So it does look as though this is an example of a Christian who became demon-filled, or perhaps I should say Satan-filled.

But there is belief and belief. The devils (demons) themselves believe — and tremble (James 2:19). They *believe* there is a God and a Christ and a Holy Spirit — in fact they know it very well! — but they have nothing that could be compared to a Christian's trust and allegiance! Ananias couldn't blame his sin on Satan; Peter said that Ananias himself had conceived his wicked idea in his own heart (5:4). And this wasn't just suddenly giving in to a temptation, as a Christian may do sometimes. The record shows that Ananias and his wife had deliberately planned the whole thing, and had even conspired together to tell the same lie so that they would not be found out (4:7-9). Think of all the evil planning this pair did, and all the action it took to carry their plans out. They agreed together to sell their property, to say they got less than they did, to turn this smaller amount over to the church, and to testify falsely to the whole thing if they were questioned independently. This was no ordinary sin. This was a wilful, deliberate, carefully-plotted sin against the church and against the Holy Spirit (5:3). No wonder Peter said that Satan had filled Ananias's heart!

I can picture Paul sinning through anger or perhaps pride. I can see Peter trembling before a servant girl and denying he knew Jesus. But I can't imagine any sincere Christian planning and conspiring to carry out the deliberate deception and spiritual theft that Ananias and Sapphira engineered. So this incident doesn't convince me at all that anyone can at any moment be filled with demons.

My friend, my prayer for you is that you will be so filled with the Holy Spirit that there will be *no room* for any evil spirits.

Satan will attack you and oppress you if he can. He attacked Job. He oppresses me sometimes. He even tempted Jesus! But I can never believe that our Father in heaven, the Father who saves us and keeps us and fills us, will let the devil get the best of us.

My prayer is that we Christians will learn to walk in *Christ's* fulness, with our feet on the ground, ready to admit our weaknesses and failures, and just as ready to seek and accept forgiveness. We need to put our complete dependence on Christ. "But if we walk in the light, as he is in the light, we have fellowship one with another, and the blood of Jesus Christ his Son cleanseth us from all sin" (1 John 1:7).

17

Beating the Devil

I get tired of hearing people say, "I don't believe in a personal devil." As this age hurtles on into demonism and all the other nightmares of the occult world, I predict that more people will *know* what the devil is like.

For me, Jesus settled the question long ago of who the devil is. He called him a liar and a murderer (John 8:44). You can't call an abstraction a liar! Jesus called Satan the father of the wicked, just as God is the Father of Christians. I've noticed that those who don't believe in a personal devil don't seem to have much notion of a personal God, either, or even very much interest in Jesus. And as you may have noticed, some of the best translations of the Bible change the words in the Lord's Prayer, "Deliver us from evil," to "Deliver us from the Evil One." The Living Bible has it that way, and so does Good News for Modern Man. The Greek scholars say that that's the best translation. If they're right, as I believe they are, Jesus wants us to pray not only for deliverance from evil in the abstract, but for deliverance from the father and leader of all the evil forces that seem to be running wild more and more in the world today. Jesus wants us to ask God for protection from a personal devil!

Let's not underestimate Satan. The Bible squares with the experience of a whole lot of Christians in showing how powerful he is. And while it's completely true that if you resist the devil, he will flee from you, I've sometimes been asked: "How do you *resist* the devil?"

As I've been writing this book I've been constantly amazed at all the things God has done to help me put it all together. People have been telling me of their occult experiences, letters have been coming in from all over, and I've been coming across more and more evidence of what is happening right now in the supernatural world. All of it fits together like the pieces of a giant jigsaw puzzle.

For example, while I was flying to Chicago recently I ran across a man whose appearance and accent told me right away that he too was from Latin America. Before long Julio Ruibal was telling me the amazing story of his life — a story that corroborates all I have found true of the occult world, and that answers the question of exactly how a person can learn to effectively resist the devil and send him flying.

"For many years," Julio told me, "I was in bondage to evil spirits. Now the Lord has translated me out of the kingdom of darkness into the Kingdom of His dear Son, praise His name!"

"You sound like you know a lot about witchcraft," I said.

"Nicky," said Julio, "I do. I am not boasting when I say that. I want to tell you about my achievements in the occult, not because they mean anything to me now that I have found the Lord, but so you will understand that I have experimental knowledge of what I am talking about. For years I was into many forms of occult 'wisdom,' as I used to call it.

"I was born in Bolivia. From the time I was six I wanted to become a doctor and be able to heal sick people. But I saw no way to make my dream come true, and by the time I was eighteen years old I had no outstanding success in anything, and everyone in my family let me know it. I tried music and sports, but I wasn't really good in either one. I felt if I couldn't change my life somehow I would be a nothing, and I just couldn't go on living.

"Now this is how the occult world appeals. It promises you what you desire. It is like a big papaya tree I once climbed. It was a hot day and I was hungry and thirsty, and I felt I just had to get some of that juicy, delicious papaya fruit I could see hanging from the limbs of the tree. I knew if I shook the tree, the fruit would probably be smashed or lost in the underbrush, so I decided I had to climb the tree. I had no doubt the big branches would hold me—but I was wrong. As I stepped out on the first branch to reach the fruit, it broke. The papaya tree had all the appearance of providing what I wanted so desperately, but it was just *appearance.* That is how the occult works.

"Deciding that occultism would bring me satisfaction and success, I studied it in many forms. I began with the occult religions of Tibet. These religions work basically with the control of the mind—astral projection, psychometry, telepathy, and astrology. Quickly mastering these, I went on to the religions of India, especially Hinduism and yoga—hatha-yoga, jnana-yoga, bhakti-yoga, and all their variations. Then I went into the occult studies of the Western Hemisphere—palmistry, tarot cards, transcendental meditation, extrasensory perception, parapsychology. Finally I studied what is supposed to be the highest discipline of all—the mysticism of prayer and worship.

"Prayer and worship sound fine, don't they? But you can pray to Satan as well as to Jesus. And you can get an answer from Satan! Of course, if you pray to any spirit but the Spirit of God or Jesus, you will have to pay a price. Satan can give a person many things— money, healing, knowledge, protection, luck. Satan is a giver—but a *dirty* giver.

"What Satan gives, I have found, he always takes back with heavy interest. He is just like a drug pusher. A pusher may give you a nice free shot of dope, and for a little while you may get what you think is a wonderful high, but those few minutes or hours are followed by torment, fear, the feeling of being lost, the desperation of not knowing what is happening to you. And the pusher makes you pay a horrible price in the end—always in money—often with your life. The Bible calls Satan the Tormentor. That is a perfect description. He gives—but finally he takes everything back, and you have to pay terrible interest."

"I know that," I said. "How well I know it! The trouble is that so many people don't know it."

"I agree 100 percent," said Julio. "I pray constantly that the eyes of more people will be opened to the devil's tricks. What I have to say next shows how well he lays his traps, and how foolishly a young person can walk into them."

Then Julio told me his amazing story.

I advanced in the occult sphere so fast that I soon became the youngest guru in the Western Hemisphere, and one of the most advanced and powerful. Twice a week I taught yoga on television. Hatha-yoga sounds like a nice simple set of exercises; everybody thinks it is just gymnastics. I want to warn that it is just the beginning of a devilish trap. After I became an instructor in hatha-yoga, my guru showed me that the only thing those exercises really do is open your appetite for the occult. They are like marihuana; they usually lead you on to a drug that is worse and stronger, binding you so completely that only Christ can deliver you.

Many people think that occult power is just the power of the mind. This is not true. There is a point beyond which the power of the mind ends and demonic power takes over. For example, astrology begins with pure astronomy — with the position of the stars and planets and various dates and angles. But there is a point where this kind of information ends and interpretation must be applied to the individual person whose horoscope you are reading. This is where the astrologer senses the need for help. This help will not come from God, for He does not want us to know the future, except as He reveals it. So this is where you open yourself to demonic influence. The demons know something about the future. Satan wants you to desire that knowledge. So here the demon steps in to provide superhuman aid in interpreting the horoscope. Up to this point I was in Bolivia. Here you see how the occult world is like that papaya tree, promising to fulfill all your dreams. While I was still in my teens, the doors all opened for me to come to the United States to study medicine. Very soon I was taking a premed course in Los Angeles, but at the same time I was doing things no normal person could do. I could hypnotize people, control them with my eyes, make them do things I willed them to do. I knew things that would happen in the future. I could cause strange things to happen. I could communicate by telepathy, even if the other person were miles away. And I could learn what I needed to without studying.

So here I was, all my dreams coming true! Truly it looked as though the occult was the key to my heart's desire. Actually, I had reached the point the Tibetans call Nirvana and the Western occultists call Absolute Knowledge. It was the point where I was so in tune with the demon world that I could know things and do things without any conscious effort. I got power and information directly from supernatural sources.

The fact is that I was sent to the United States to help set up the first legal occult medical center in this country. I was part of the hierarchy of the leading occult organization of the whole Western Hemisphere. In fact, two months after I came to America, I received a letter from my guru in Bolivia telling me that the guru over him had died, and so my own guru and I had in our hands the responsibility for the teaching of yoga in its deepest form throughout the West.

My guru went under the name of Nero. I had the occult name of Parrot. The two of us were now the only persons outside the East with so much power and knowledge. So I am a walking testimony to the wonderful power of Jesus. If He could convert me, He can change anyone!

The work I now did was dangerous and complicated. In a few months I had trained about fifteen students to the point where they could teach and study at the same time.

When I came to America I wanted to know what was going on in the occult here, so I talked to different gurus in many different areas of the United States. I found out they didn't know anything! Compared to what I had learned, they were raw novices. I remember when one guru came to my house in Los Angeles and my students gave a demonstration of what they had learned. It just blew this man's mind that I had taught them so much while I was so young.

While I took my premedical training I was giving occult lectures in different schools, high schools, and colleges.

Everything was going my way. But you know, the devil is not like the Lord. Under the devil you never know when the magic may backfire and things may fall apart. This was what happened to me next. All of a sudden things started to happen that I did not understand. There were strange problems among my students. Divisions sprang up between them. Some of my students decided to drop out of the classes in yoga. One of the students was a Jewish student named Aaron.

I had such complete control over my students that when Aaron came to tell me he had decided to quit, he was crying and fearful. In fact, I was sometimes called a second Charles Manson because of my power over my students. The New York Mau Maus were rough with knives and guns. We were rough with something much worse and more fearful — demonic power. So when Aaron got out that he didn't want to learn any more of the occult, I surprised him by answering, "I'm glad."

I surprised myself, too, for the strange thing was that I was truly glad, somehow, that Aaron was not going further into the occult. I felt a sudden sense of joy that he was getting out.

Other students decided to drop out, too, and all of a sudden there were the strangest tensions and difficulties in the work. The weirdest things happened, which I won't take time now to go into. Let me just say that my nerves were terribly disturbed, and the pains I had been getting ever since I started into the occult got worse.

Within a month I had to go to the doctors. They gave me some pills but said they could not find anything wrong with me.

But I was beginning to feel very weak and helpless. The way people sometimes know such things, I knew inside that I was dying—yes, *dying.* I can't tell you how I knew it, but I knew it. When a man is dying you expect him to get in touch with his friends. I didn't have any friends; I had been too busy for friends. I did have my students. I called an emergency meeting of my students and I was so weak they had to carry me to my bed. I was still in my teens, and I was dying. The students asked me if I wanted a priest. No, I said, I didn't want anybody. I just wanted to die in peace. The students played a record they knew I liked, I said good-bye, wrote a farewell note, and lay down to die.

I felt the shadow of death. It was not a peaceful feeling! It was a strong, ugly feeling. A feeling of everlasting condemnation.

I tried to take hold of the promises of the occult world. I thought about the reincarnation I had been taught all about. I told myself that my mission in this life was over and I must get ready for the next existence. Because of my occult progress I should have been prepared for a much better life the next time—but all of a sudden the thought didn't make any sense.

I felt I was sliding down into a place too awful for words. I had believed I was fortified against death with my special knowledge and powers. But at that point everything around me felt like those papaya branches—everything seemed to be breaking up, and what I had thought was within my reach suddenly disappeared. I felt I was falling, falling—then I wasn't conscious of anything more.

Next morning I opened my eyes to find my students all around me. They had stayed up all night praying for me. We had so many gods in our occult studies, I don't know who all they had prayed to, but I'm sure of one thing: Someone had prayed to Jesus, and He in His amazing grace had answered that prayer.

I opened my eyes and I heard a voice speaking in my heart. I didn't know what that voice was then, although I know now that it was the Lord. He was saying:

Julio, you have one more chance, and that is all.

I wondered what it meant — whether it was my conscience or my sub-conscious trying to give me a message. But I knew I had better listen.

I slowed down. I stopped teaching and let my students take care of the work. I slowed and slowed until the work was almost dissolved.

I told my students: "From now on we are doing something different. We will not have the instruction any more. Each of you will continue your studies on your own."

As I was dismantling the work I had labored so hard to build up, I felt power working through me that was new and different. I thought this was the power of my mind but I was wrong. I remember that when I was re-leasing the students, I told them, "You are free," and I felt a great relief. I, too, felt free. Something was working within me that was different from anything I had experienced before, causing me to joyfully undo all I had been doing. Naturally, the devil didn't like it!

I felt low. The headaches I had been having came back worse than ever and everything was terrible. All of a sudden I was financially broke. Things got worse and worse and worse.

One day I was at school with my books on my arm when a girl went past wearing a poncho. The poncho looked familiar and when this girl came back, passing very close to where I was standing, I asked her, "Is that poncho from Bolivia?"

I don't know why I asked that. The thought just came into my mind, all of a sudden, to speak to this girl. This girl — I discovered later her name was Cathy — this girl stopped and smiled. She answered my question: "Yes."

Now I am not a timid person. Usually I have no difficulty talking to any-one, but at that moment something froze my tongue and I couldn't say a word. Finally Cathy walked away.

Then something happened to me. Some friends were nearby. They used to be my students, but now they were no longer under my control and they were becoming my friends. I said to them, "I'm going to run after her."

One of the students said, "You don't do that in America!"

I said, "I don't care what you do in America!" I threw my books down on the campus — I remember there were some occult books I was holding, along with some chemistry and medical books — and I ran.

I wasn't really running after Cathy. Cathy is a nice girl, but she never

became my girl friend. I was really running after Jesus. What attracted me
to Cathy was Jesus in her. As I threw down my books I was saying to the
world, "I don't care what you think, and I'm through with the things you
think are important." It was just like hearing Jesus call, "Follow me," and
giving up everything to do that.

I ran for almost a block. I almost missed Cathy, but finally I caught sight
of her and caught up with her. I said: "Excuse me. Ah—I don't know—I
hope you don't think I was making fun of you or anything like that."

Cathy asked, "How did you know I am a believer?"

I started to freeze again. I was aware of something happening that was
completely beyond my control. I said, "I didn't know you were a believer."

"Then why," asked Cathy, "did you ask me if I was a believer?"

Truly the Lord was working a miracle! When I asked Cathy, "Is that
poncho from Bolivia?" I was no more than three yards away from her. I
know I have an accent, but not so bad an accent that what I asked could
sound like "Are you a believer?" I remember that I had pointed to Cathy's
poncho as I asked my question.

But God had let Cathy hear, not what my mouth was saying, but what my
heart was asking. When I got into the occult I was searching desperately
for I didn't know what. Now I know that underneath it all I was searching
for God. I remember that one day I had decided I would fast until I literally
saw God. I guess I expected Him to walk into the room physically and say,
"Hello, Julio, how are you doing?" But of course it would not work; to see
God, first you must believe. Yet even though I did not know that then, I
was looking for that Someone who leaves our hearts hungry until we
feed on Him.

So now I asked Cathy, "*Are* you a believer?"

"Yes," she said. "Are you?"

"Well, yes," I said, "I am a believer." Cathy didn't ask me *what* I believed. At that time I believed all kinds of things, true and false.

Next day Cathy and I went for a walk. I started to tell her all about the
occult, although I didn't call it the occult because I didn't know that. I
didn't even know that I was working for the devil. At that point I didn't
even believe that the devil existed. I believed that there is a negative force
in life that fights against the positive forces. The first trick of the devil is
to make you believe there is no devil.

Cathy listened to everything I said and finally she invited me to go to a
religious service with her. I asked if my guru could come, and we went.

The service was being conducted by Kathryn Kuhlman. As my guru and

I listened—I had to translate a lot of it so the guru could understand—we sensed a power different from anything we had ever known. And we saw that power at work.

When we saw people being delivered from all kinds of sickness and problems, we blew our minds. All around us people were getting visibly healed and *healed* and HEALED! We did not believe that such a thing was possible. For the first time the real and true power of God, the power of the Holy Spirit, got through to both of us.

I had been working in healing before I came to the Lord. I searched desperately for things to help the sick—hypnotism, magnetism, all kinds of psychic therapy—but it wouldn't work. Some of us did get a few small results once in a while. I would hear that a certain guru had healed someone of cancer, and I thought that was marvelous. I tried to do something similar, but I never was able to. The devil may heal someone once in a while because what he really wants, and will do anything to get, is that person's soul, but healing is really against his nature, just as it is the essence of God's nature to heal and restore.

Seeing people really healed in Kathryn Kuhlman's services deeply touched my heart. I had stepped into a new dimension, as different from anything I had known as stepping into a completely different world. The Spirit of God began to work within me. Softly, softly He worked, breaking down my resistance, showing me His love and power.

After the service I had such complicated, mixed-up feelings! I didn't know what to think about it all, and neither did my guru. We had seen so many people healed and transformed. And something had happened to me, too. For a long time my back had bothered me. Right there during the service I knew that my back was healed. It stayed healed, too, which proves that God does not always heal you because you have faith; He may heal you to show you how much He loves you!

The next day both of us went to a small prayer meeting. There were about fifteen people there. They all got down on their knees and everyone prayed and prayed. I prayed, too—I believed in all kinds of spirits and powers, and I prayed to them all. Fortunately, no one there realized how far from the truth I was, or if they did hear what I was saying, they didn't let on that I was making pagan prayers to false gods, and they just prayed for me anyway.

After about an hour there were only about ten people still there. They were laying their hands on anyone who wanted prayer. I was still having those headaches, so I said to myself, "I might as well try it." Then I said to the Christians, "Okay, you can pray for me."

I sat down in the chair where they laid their hands on whoever wanted prayer, and everybody gathered around. They were young people and older people and middle-aged people.

As they stood around me and started to put their hands on my head, something started to happen. I had tremendous emotions in my soul, and there seemed to be a great commotion in the room. An explosive tension was starting to build up.

I know now that the Spirit of God was beginning to expose the things so deeply embedded in my soul — yoga, clairvoyance, astrology, voodoo, belief in reincarnation, the Kabbala, levitation, metaphysical healing, automatic writing, use of the pendulum, extrasensory perception, and all the rest! The powers of darkness within me were coming face to face with the power of God. God was challenging the Evil One, and I was the battlefield. I sensed that each one of those occult things was represented by a different demon that had taken hold of my soul.

There were some people present who didn't realize what was going on and finally left. But there were two ladies, mature in the Spirit, who discerned the demons inside me and stayed with me. It was just as though the Holy Spirit had said, "Get out and let Me take care of this."

My body was shaking and the room was spinning around me. I felt what seemed like a warm electric current coursing all through me and it made my body numb. It seemed like the Lord was giving me an anesthetic before an operation. I truly believe that He did so to prevent the demons inside me from harming me when they were expelled.

The two ladies were experienced in delivering demon-possessed persons from satanic power. One of them sat down on the sofa as though she was simply waiting to see what the Lord would do. The other lady walked toward me — led, as I now know, by the Spirit of God — and as she did this I felt the power of God coming into my body. It came into my head like thunder breaking. It passed through my head, through my neck and back. I was thrown out of the chair. I fell flat on the floor and lay there as though I was nailed down.

Somehow I lifted up both arms. I had never before in my life lifted up my arms to God. I could feel the demons going out of me. It seemed as if my head was broken.

At the same time as I felt the demons leaving like an electric current shooting through my body, I felt something else. It seemed like a shock of thunder coming in and shaking my whole body. I started crying out in languages I didn't understand. I was being filled with the Holy Spirit and speaking in tongues! For nearly an hour I was crying, shaking, lifting up my hands, and feeling the tremendous power that was filling me.

Of course, at first I did not understand what was happening. Then some-one came into the room and exclaimed, "You have been delivered! You are being filled with the Spirit!" Later I wondered how this could be happen-ing if I did not understand it was happening. But the Bible says that God knows the desires of our hearts. After all my years of fruitless searching for God, it was *He* who found *me!*

You may think this is the end of the story, but it is just the beginning. The next day Cathy explained to me that I would have to renounce all my occult practices. It took me a while to realize that this was true. I had al-ready renounced some things I knew were wrong, but some of the other occult things were still in me. I finally realized that I had to renounce each occult practice or belief, one by one, so that the spirit of each one could be cast out until every last one was gone.

A few weeks later I was able to deliver my guru from bondage to all the demons within him. We both came to see that anyone who has been in-volved in the occult had to do three things about each occult practice: confess aloud the sin; renounce it; and in the authority of Christ pray and command each demon to get out. It is good to have someone pray for you as you do this, but you yourself can command the demons to leave in the power of the name of the Lord.

My guru and I realized that we had to burn all our occult books, just like in Acts 19. It was not easy, believe me, after we had been studying and living by these things for so long. We had tapes, books, pictures — occult materials worth thousands and thousands of dollars. As we were throwing them into the fire in the middle of the night, I looked through the flames at my guru on the other side. I could see the tears shining in his eyes. I went to him and said, "I know, Nero, it hurts me too." But we were not hurt by the price of all those things in the flames; we were hurt because we had been so terribly fooled.

"Julio," Nero said, "I must go back to South America. My wife, my children, my relatives, and hundreds of people down there got involved in the occult through me. I've got to go back and bring them to Christ."

When I had told my students that all the things I had been teaching them were from the devil, they had become bitter against me, and for a time I had felt bitter against my guru. It was a heavy thing to know that we had been preaching doctrines of the devil. But as we burned the books and tapes and pictures, the peace of God came upon us and the bitterness disappeared.

After we burned the occult books, the Lord led me to help my former students one by one until most of them were delivered. One by one they were saved and baptized until they got the blessings He had given me. It was amazing to see how He worked.

Now I want to emphasize something! The deliverance part is nothing! The hard part is to *keep* delivered. Soon life for me began to be hard, painful, confusing. All the memories, all the complicated occult ideas kept coming back into my mind and I had to rebuke them and rebuke them and *rebuke* them.

The warfare with Satan got very heavy. I felt his attacks. I know how he works. There may be fears, loneliness, feelings of separation, desperation, even suicide, and much more. I could feel the demons coming back.

Nero felt it, too, and we went to prayer meetings every day to pray and ask prayer. It was so frightening. I got desperate. I would come home at night and feel the devil trying to terrify me. I knew he didn't want to lose me. I heard him say, "Either you are mine or you are nobody's."

I knew the devil wanted to kill me. He tried to drive me insane through the different things that came into my mind — the desperation and confusion. Truly he did his best to scare me — back into his power. Some nights I would go to bed and I could feel the furniture in my room moving. I heard people walking around when I knew no one was there and I could feel my heart beating faster and faster. I had to keep lifting up the name of Jesus until the demons went away.

I read what the Bible says about Satan: "Be sober, be vigilant; because your adversary the devil, as a roaring lion, walketh about, seeking whom he may devour: whom resist stedfast in the faith . . ." (1 Peter 5:8, 9). And I said, "I have no faith, I cannot believe any more. I have been so deceived before, how do I know *this* is the truth?" As you can see, there was great confusion in my mind.

But Peter goes on to say, "Whom resist stedfast in the faith, knowing that the same afflictions are accomplished. . . . But the God of all grace, who has called us unto his eternal glory by Christ Jesus, after that ye have suffered awhile, make you perfect, establish, strengthen, settle you" (vs. 9, 10). As the attacks continued, I found that I was slowly becoming strengthened. The more I called on the Lord, the more I was able to stand on my feet and fight the devil. I got stronger and stronger. The Lord settled me, perfected and established and confirmed me in His truth.

I devoured the Bible and learned the whole truth about Satan and all his works. After awhile when I would come home and be attacked again, with the bed shaking and the furniture moving, I would just lie down on the bed and say: "Thank you, Jesus! Glory to God! Lord, I worship You!" And He gave me peace and quiet, just as He promised.

Then there had to be healing of my memories. As I prayed, and as my Christian friends prayed for me, and as I read God's Word and witnessed for Him, the healing took place. The old memories of all the things of the evil world slowly lost their sting. When I thought of them, I was able to thank God for His redemption.

I have told you how I used to dream of being a doctor. When I found the Lord I gave up everything I was doing, including my premedical studies. I gave my whole life to Him. After awhile I found myself praying for people who were sick — and they would be healed! The Lord gave me back my dream, and fulfilled it in a way better than I could have hoped or thought!

"Julio," I said, when he finished his story, "what you've told me today is going to help people you will never see until you get to heaven."

"When you write your book," Julio called after me as I dashed for my plane, "tell them that the demons do have power. But they use their powers just to get people stoned, to keep them from seeing their real problems. When I was in yoga I had some truly frightening powers. But all of them are *nothing* compared to what God can do. Praise His name!"

I praise God too when I think of the amazing change in this young man who once led others into the occult. I must have talked with Julio for three or four hours altogether. I asked him if he would record his testimony on tape and send it to me so I could include it in this book, and he graciously did so. However, I would like to share with you what Julio said at the very beginning of the recording. Here it is, just as it came off the tape:

> *Nicky, I have never had such hassles in my whole life. I have made many tapes, but never with troubles like this. Every time I have tried to record my testimony for you, something has happened. One time the dog chewed up the wire to the microphone! But with the help of God I am finally getting it all down.*

That reminds me of Mr. Benson and Lana and Lou Rawls. They (Lou and Lana), too, put their story on tape — but the first tape recorder they tried refused to record properly, the second would not work, and they had to get a third before they could get the story all down. After they finally got their tape finished and mailed it off, insured special delivery, it came back to them water-soaked and ruined. My address had been ripped off the package. The post office sent it back to Lou and Lana because their name and address were still intact in one corner of the ruined package. So the two of them sat down once more and did the tape all over again. This last time it came through safely, thank God!

One message that comes through to me loud and clear from all this is: Faith and persistence pay off. If you just hang in there long enough, you'll make it. To put it another way:

And let us not be weary in well doing: for in due season we shall reap, if we faint not.   Galatians 6:9

18

How To Be Safe

"We go by our horoscopes all the time," two stewardesses told me as I talked with them about the occult. "Surely you don't think there's anything wrong with reading the astrology columns, do you?"

I have to admit that it may look harmless enough. But it's part of the whole occult package that God condemns from beginning to end of the Bible. As I've tried to show, any part of the occult can easily lead to the rest, and it's a dangerous business to get into any part of it.

You don't have to take just my word for that. Even if what the Bible says is left out of it, there are the warnings of the occultists themselves. The occult expert G. de Purucker, for example, warns about yoga in *Occult Glossary* published by Theosophical University Press: ". . . dangers lurk at every step, and the meddler in these things is likely to bring disaster upon himself, both in matters of health and as regards sane mental equilibrium." And about hypnotism: "This is in nine hundred and ninety-nine times out of a thousand a wrong thing to do. . . ." That's from a man who spent a lifetime studying Eastern philosophies, theosophy, and the whole field of the occult, and he should know.

The witch Sarah Lyddon Morrison warns: "Any power that's

used unjudiciously, haphazardly, and without careful thought eventually snarls back around the user and trips him up. . . . If we cause disorder with misused power, we become vulnerable to all manner of terrible repercussions." *The Witches' Almanac* says: "Once you begin to explore your psychic perception you have entered a path of no return." (*The Witches' Almanac,* published by Grosset and Dunlap, is prepared and edited by Elizabeth Pepper and John Wilcock.)

A man named G. H. Estabrooks was in a military hospital when he decided to do some mental experiments to help pass the time. Working with autosuggestion, he got to the point where he could count to five and "see" a polar bear which would respond to his mental commands. He could make it march around the hospital ward, kiss the nurses, and even jump out the hospital window. The trouble was that the bear appeared when Estabrooks did not want it to, and would not go away. At night it sometimes jumped out from a dark corner at him, or startled him by showing up where he least expected to find a wild animal. He finally got rid of it after undergoing a whole month of mental therapy, but until that point it greatly troubled his mind. (This incident is from *Unfinished Man* by Raymond Van Over, published by World Publishing Company.)

And when so many people are experimenting with the mind today, I wish they realized these dangers that are so well known to those who have specialized in these areas. Suppose you don't believe in a real spiritual world and you attribute everything psychic to mental suggestion or imagination. Even if that's all there is to it, you are getting onto very thin ice when you dabble in psychic things — as G. H. Estabrooks learned.

Today there is a young woman in a mental institution near Baltimore, Maryland, whose mysterious malady has been called "one of the most bizarre in modern witchcraft." A perfectly normal girl until a few years ago, Barbara started reading about witchcraft in the sixteenth century and decided to do an experiment. One evening in November, 1968, she made a magic circle, lit four candles, and began a witch's rite with her pet cat in her arms. At first nothing happened except that the cat, Margot, meowed as though frightened. Then, according to a diary in which Barbara recorded her experiments, the cat became strangely quiet—and soon Barbara felt that she was in Margot's body and Margot in hers. Barbara roamed the streets of Baltimore inside the body of her cat until she got back home and somehow returned to her own body.

Increasingly obsessed by witchcraft, according to her diary, Barbara practiced her lycanthropy spell until she could apparently enter her pet cat's body whenever she wished. Then, one night, something happened that no one understands. Barbara worked her spell—and two days later a neighbor called the janitor because the continual meowing in Barbara's apartment disturbed him. Opening the door, the janitor found inside the apartment not Barbara's cat but Barbara—behaving and meowing like a cat.

It was theorized that when Barbara was in the streets inside Margot's furry body, a truck rolled over the body of the cat, leaving Barbara's spirit without a dwelling place and Margot's presence back in the apartment inside the body of Barbara. Whatever had happened, according to Emile C. Schurmacher who reports the case of Barbara and Margot in the book *Witchcraft in America Today*, Barbara today never says a human word. She purrs and meows, laps up milk from a saucer, and eats pieces of fish from the floor on her hands and knees. When she is angry she claws and bites like a cat.

While I was finishing this book the occult movie *The Exorcist* was being filmed in Washington, D.C., and New York. Few people who see the movie or read the book from which it was made—a national best seller—may know that the story is based on an actual case of demon possession. Noises that could not be explained were heard in a house in the state of Washington. While a fourteen-year-old boy in the house was sleeping his bed repeatedly crept across the floor. A priest was brought to the house to drive out the demon through the rite of exorcism. During the rite, the boy screamed, cursed, and spoke in Latin, a language he knew nothing about.

An ominous fact in this connection is this: During the filming of *The Exorcist*, a twelve-year-old girl in the city manifested symptoms very much like those of the demon-possessed child in the film. The girl finally admitted having read the book. How many other cases of demon possession, imaginary or actual, will erupt before America's occult kick is over?

J. Stafford Wright tells of a Christian gathering at which some-one suggested holding a seance. One young man who was present had previously taken part in a seance, and at the very mention of the word *seance,* an evil spirit attacked the boy violently.

A few years ago an Arab boy spent many hours studying mysti-cism and mental power. According to *Time Magazine* (April 4, 1969), he read courses in Rosicrucianism by candlelight in front of a mirror. Once he looked into the mirror and saw there, in place of his own intense face, the face of Robert Kennedy. He decided Kennedy must die, and at the next opportunity Sirhan Sirhan shot and killed the famous Senator.

As the twentieth century hurtles toward its end, I believe we are going to see stranger and stranger things. In 2 Thessalonians there is a remarkable passage about the return of Christ:

". . . that day shall not come, except there come a falling away first, and that man of sin be revealed, the son of perdition; Who opposeth and exalteth himself above all that is called God, or that is worshiped: so that he as God sitteth in the temple of God, shew-ing himself that he is God" (2:3, 4).

Paul is saying that Christ will not come again until there is first a falling away. "Falling away" may mean either a falling away from the Christian faith or a great final rebellion — or both. Who is the man of sin who will be revealed before Christ returns? Notice that he is called "the son of perdition" and will proclaim that he is God and will oppose God and exalt himself above Him.

There are many different interpretations of Bible passages such as these and I don't want to get into a discussion of them. What im-presses me is how this fits in with what we are already seeing hap-pening. Rebellion and unbelief are everywhere. It is fashionable and hip to oppose God and everything related to God. And already Satan himself is worshiped in place of God in so-called churches of Satan, while the devil and his angels are invoked in witchcraft covens all around the world.

Paul goes on: "For the mystery of iniquity doth already work: only he who now letteth will let, until he be taken out of the way. And then shall that Wicked be revealed, whom the Lord shall con-sume with the spirit of his mouth, and shall destroy with the brightness of his coming: Even him, whose coming is after the working of Satan with all power and signs and lying wonders, And with all deceivableness of unrighteousness in them that perish; because they received not the love of the truth, that they might be saved" (vs. 7–10).

I like the way the Living Bible translates that:

As for the work this man of rebellion and hell will do when he comes, it is already going on, but he himself will not come until the one who is holding him back steps out of the way. Then this wicked one will appear, whom the Lord Jesus will burn up with the breath of his mouth and destroy by his presence when he returns. This man of sin will come as Satan's tool, full of satanic power, and will trick everyone with strange demonstrations, and will do great miracles. He will completely fool those who are on their way to hell because they have said "no" to the Truth; they have refused to believe it and love it, and let it save them.

The wicked one who is coming will carry on a work that had already begun in the time of the New Testament. But through the ages God has been holding Satan back. At the end of this age, He will step out of the way and for a few years a man full of sin, a tool of Satan with satanic power, will fool everyone who does not really believe and love God's saving truth. Such people will believe lies and strong delusions. (See verse 11.)

All this looks like the occult to me. What else is filled with deception, delusions, and demonstrations of seemingly miraculous power? As this age rolls on, I believe such demonstrations will become more and more convincing to everyone but those who are close to Jesus.

I predict that in a short time another new religion will sweep across much of the world. Maybe it will be a mixture of witchcraft, spiritualism, and some Eastern religion. It wouldn't surprise me if it had elements of Christianity in it. That way it would fool a lot of half-committed Christians. What shape it will take exactly I don't know, but I feel sure that the time is ripe for some new delusion.

The only ones who will be completely safe in the times ahead of us are the Christians who love Jesus and live 100 percent for Him. All others will become easy prey for that old serpent who has been a liar and murderer from the beginning of time.

And we've got to be all-out for Jesus Christ. There is a new religion that is becoming popular in Puerto Rico today. In this religion there is a woman now dead whose spirit is worshipped; she is supposed to give guidance to the worshipers. Luis Rosario was telling me about a Christian lady who was urged to pray to God to see if she shouldn't try this religion. Luis told this lady, "If you pray that way, you will probably hear a voice telling you to follow that religion. You shouldn't even ask whether such a religion is right." I agree completely. *Don't even ask* if you should look into any religion that differs in any way from what God says in the Bible. Have nothing to do with anything different from the gospel.

Any day now you will be hearing about some new religion that may sound very attractive. Don't be surprised. Satan knows how to look like an angel of light (2 Corinthians 11:14). The next time you hear of a new gospel, remember this: "If . . . an angel from heaven, should preach to you a gospel that is different from the one we preached to you, may he be condemned to hell" (Galatians 1:8 TEV)!

The times are coming when there will be false prophets and false Christs, false spiritual leaders who will use great signs and wonders to attract followers, so they will almost be able to deceive the very people of God. Jesus predicted that in Matthew 24:24.

When you begin to see such things, don't say you were never warned!

My study of the occult has convinced me that the devil and evil spirits and practitioners of the occult have real power. But even though Satan's power is unleashed more than ever in the days ahead, I don't believe that Christians should live in fear. We are covered by Jesus' blood! His blood is a shield that protects us completely. Once Satan even tried to take over Jesus, but He never gave in one moment. The devil had no power over Jesus and he has no power over anyone who trusts completely in Him.

In the Book of Job, you remember, Satan went to the Lord to get permission to put Job through many trials so that he would curse and renounce God. The Lord said, in effect, "Job is in your hands to do with as you wish, but you cannot touch his soul" (Job 2:6). Now Job was in love with God and trusted Him completely. He went through many trials, but they were used to bring him closer to the Lord, so he could say at the end, "I have heard of thee by the hearing of the ear, but now mine eye seeth thee" (42:5).

Remember that Satan can never do a thing to you that God doesn't permit for your good — every test and trial can bring you closer to Him and teach you to know Him better.

19

God Can Still Work Miracles

The alarm clock went off at 6:15 that dark Friday morning recently. As I pushed the blanket back and turned off the alarm, I thought, *Oh, no—here I go again.*

I felt glum as I showered and shaved. To be honest, I have to admit that I often get tired of traveling. I fly about 150,000 miles a year, and after a while an itinerary like that wears you down. It's hardest of all when I have to rush from the airport straight to the pulpit. When that happens, as it does so often during my youth crusades, I sometimes feel beat before I start.

Gloria must have read my thoughts, for she squeezed my hand as she poured me a cup of coffee. "You are helping many people find Jesus, Nicky," she said.

"I know," I nodded. Bringing people to Him is the great thing about the crusades that take up so many of my weekends. But as I grabbed the bags I had packed the night before and got in my car, I still felt blue.

And as I drove to the Raleigh airport I became aware of a familiar hang-up. The smell of the traffic exhaust and jet fumes irritated my nostrils, and the roar of cars and taxis and planes taking off grated on my eardrums. I asked myself: *Is it worth all this*

*rush and strain? Why do I keep knocking myself out? Isn't there
some easier way to serve the Lord?*

My plane took off at eight and landed at Chicago at 8:44. The connecting flight left at 10:10 A.M. and reached Salt Lake City at 12:20. I left there at 1:48 on a Frontier Airlines plane, arriving at just about three o'clock in Rock Spring, Wyoming, where I was scheduled for a two-day crusade.

A group of lively teen-agers and a beautiful Christian lady gave me a warm welcome at the Rock Springs airport. That was quite a contrast to the rest of the day. While I ate a sandwich in a coffee shop I couldn't help hearing the loud debate at the next table. A bald gentleman was saying, "That Floyd Little! He's not a big player, but when he gets out on a football field how he can run!"

A thin man with a waxy moustache shook his head: "Roman Gabriel is the one I'm betting on. He's going to put the Rams on top this year, you see if he doesn't." Two other men at the table both chimed in at the same time, one insisting that Fran Tarkenton was the greatest football player in the country, the other man rooting for Joe Namath.

I'm not against sports, but I couldn't help thinking as the men argued: *If only they would get that enthusiastic about the battle between Christ and Satan!*

Before I left the coffee shop I introduced myself to the football fans. "Good for you!" the bald man said when he learned why I was in Rock Springs. "A lot of people need preachers like you. Myself, I've got a bridge game tonight so I won't be at your meeting, but I go to church and I try to live by the Golden Rule."

I felt depressed as I got ready for the crusade. So many people seem to think that if they go to church or act nice to their neighbors, they don't need Christ! There was a fair-sized audience at the crusade that night and the next one, but I couldn't help thinking of the people who hadn't come to either meeting. How many of the empty seats in the auditorium represented men and women who thought that somehow they could work their way into heaven by their own good intentions?

Still, although it makes no real difference to me whether I'm speaking to five hundred people or twenty thousand, I was thrilled at the fantastic response on both nights to the gospel invitation. When many young people and older ones too crowded forward to accept Christ, I felt, as I often do at such times, that my heart would burst.

The next morning I got up early to fly to South Bend, Indiana. As we flew over the western prairies I talked with the woman in the seat next to me. When I told her something about the book I am writing, she bristled like an angry cat. "I can't believe in demons and devils," she said. "And even if you were right, would a good God torment such beings in hell? I wouldn't be that mean myself."

"Lady," I said, "I don't *believe* in demons, I *know* they are real. And I wouldn't call it mean to leave them to the evil they love. But it's not up to you or me to judge God. He is the Judge. One thing I'm sure of: There is no condemnation for those who are in Christ Jesus!"

The woman turned away, pushed her call button angrily, and when the stewardess appeared she ordered a double martini. She didn't speak to me again.

I was very tired when my plane touched down at South Bend. But I was encouraged by the Christian men and women who were there to meet me and drive me to the town in Michigan where I was booked to give my testimony at a county fair. And I was deeply touched when Edward Grayling and his wife invited me to rest in their home during the two hours that remained before the meeting.

I couldn't rest. I had to be by myself before I spoke at the fair. Grateful for the woods that stretched up a long sloping hill behind the Graylings' home, I plunged into the trees, exulting in the fresh air and the singing of lots of birds.

Sometimes before I preach I feel like I'm standing on a snow-covered mountain with the snow beginning to melt and rush down into streams and rivers that empty into the ocean. I sense the potential of God to use my words to bring parched souls the water of life. But this time I was the one who needed that water. I felt spiritually exhausted. I felt like a long-distance runner with the sun beating down on his head and a tremendous thirst for a long drink of cold water. I could have said with David in Psalm 42:1: "As the hart panteth after the water brooks, so panteth my soul after thee,

O God." All week I had been on the go, and now I rejoiced that I could be alone with God and the beauties of nature which He had created.

"O God," I said, "I am so tired. In two hours I am going to be standing on that platform at the fair in front of thousands of people. I don't know who will be there, but I want to do my best for You. It's such a miracle to see different ones coming forward to You, Lord. Yet I feel so dry. I've given my testimony so many times, sometimes it seems almost mechanical. Forgive me, Lord; don't let me ever be like a machine. Please help me to feel once more tonight the wonder of what You have done in my life as I tell my story. Let it come out fresh and meaningful. Give me Your power. And please, Lord, show me that You're there tonight."

I felt broken before God. Two or three mosquitoes bit me but I hardly felt them. I poured out my fears and mistakes and hang-ups. I asked Jesus to correct the things in my life that were not pleasing to Him.

Peace and joy began filling my heart. I felt the Lord's assurance that nothing done in His name is useless. The depression and discouragement that had been dogging me for so long began disappearing in the warmth of a wonderful sense of the loving presence of my Father in heaven.

I knew that Satan was on the run. And as I drank in the wonderful country atmosphere, an answer came to me for the question that woman had asked me on the flight to South Bend: "Would a good God torment such beings in hell?"

God *doesn't* torment, I realized. He lets His creatures choose life or death, blessing or cursing, as He has made clear so many times. God makes the air and the sunshine. It is man and Satan that pollute and destroy. I remembered a party I went to when I was with the gangs in Brooklyn. The air inside the crowded room was so thick with the stench of pot and tobacco and rum, walking into it was like stepping into hell. None of us had to be at that party. We had created that filthy air ourselves; we had freely chosen to breathe it.

And Satan, created for a position of great authority in heaven, chose hell. If he and his angels prefer eternal death to everlasting life, God is not going to stand in their way. God gives all of us the freedom to choose whether we want to spend time and eternity with Him or without Him. Satan and his followers have already made their choice.

While the cool breezes rustled through the leaves of the trees all around me there in the Michigan woods, I thought of the wonders of God. Satan has his signs and marvels, but God performs genuine, lasting miracles. I thought of Luis Rosario and all the others I have known whom God has saved from a living hell and molded into strong, beautiful personalities. I thought of all the little things that make life worthwhile, and God's invisible miracles everywhere, healing and helping and encouraging and inspiring His children in so many, many ways. I rejoiced in Jesus' promise: ". . . All power is given unto me in heaven and in earth . . . and, lo, I am with you alway, even unto the end of the world" (Matthew 28:18, 20).

I talked to the Lord there in the woods for a long time. Suddenly I noticed the sky was turning gray. Lightning flashed and there was a distant boom of thunder like the sound of a street rumble. It looked as though there was going to be a bad storm.

I hurried back to the house and rode with the Graylings to the fair grounds. Three thousand people had been expected for the meeting, but the grounds were packed. A police lieutenant said, "There are about seven thousand people here."

They filled the big open-air amphitheater and stood in the aisles. Soon after the service began, with lively gospel music provided by three local churches, rain began to fall. I thought to myself that there was no way we would be able to make it through the service. The rain increased from a mist to a drizzle. Raw gusts of wind roared through the bleachers, and the rain became a tremendous downpour. Lightning flashed, thunder boomed, and I felt that we were getting a preview of World War III.

The people were getting soaked through. I looked at that patient multitude and thanked God. I knew there were some beautiful Christians in the audience with great faith. I asked the Lord to take control. Then I asked the people to join with me in prayer.

"Lord," I said, "there are people here tonight who love You. There are people here who need Your help. There are many powers up there in the heavens, Lord, but You control them! All power in heaven and earth is in Your hands. You have the power to stop this storm until this service is over. We ask You to stop it. Amen."

Almost as soon as I said "Amen" the rain stopped. Amazement and delight spread over the faces in front of me. The crowd understood that God really answers prayer! The way was prepared for many to accept their supernatural Saviour. And my own faith was stirred. I said in my heart, "Thank You, Father."

I have never had an experience like that. As I told the old, old story of Jesus and His love, I saw radiant smiles breaking out on faces glistening with rain. There were women in front of me with their hair plastered down all over their heads in dripping locks. Men in expensive suits looked like Bowery bums who had slept in puddles. But it was evident that God was among us; I felt His presence and His concern for everyone there.

When I asked those who wanted to follow Christ to come forward, I was amazed at the number who responded. Their shoes squished with water as they came down the aisles, their clothes dripped, but there was a spirit of expectancy and faith I have seldom seen.

As the service ended and counselors went to the counseling rooms with the new converts, another flash of lightning split the sky and the thunder boomed in a deafening blast. Again the rain descended in torrents while people raced for their cars and the wind roared louder than ever. An announcement came over the fair's loudspeakers that a tornado was coming in our direction. Once more Mother Nature went about her business. But in between the downpours, God had kept His schedule! Thousands of people knew that night that He was on His throne.

How glad I am that I'm on Jesus' turf. I am covered by His protecting blood, and the devil can never touch my soul!

People get into the occult because they want more security, or want to know the future. Well, I couldn't ask for any more security than I've got. I know everything in the future that's important, and you can too! Demon power is real, but God is *omnipotent!* Praise Him!

Jesus offers us eternal protection and blessing. He will reign until every power in the universe is under His feet. At the moment

Satan has vast powers. He can do lying wonders and fabricate mighty delusions. But I know where he is headed with all his angels of darkness. I know that murderer and liar and destroyer, the enemy of my soul and all souls, is going to receive the punishment he deserves from a just God.

So I close these pages with the words:

To Hell with the devil!